"I have spent my entire career in th[...] kids happy. But in this insightful, [...] Katherine Koonce shows what real [...] children in today's world."

MARK BUTTON
Cofounder of The KOOSH Ball Toy Company
Author of *The Letter Box,* Surviving parent of three

"Being a parent is the great privilege of putting my handprint on another person's life. What a rewarding and yet terrifying opportunity! I am so thankful for this kind of resource to help navigate the waters through parenthood. *Parenting the Way God Parents* is refreshingly free of formulas, and packed full of wisdom and valuable insight. I will reread it for myself and recommend it again and again in my practice."

DAVID THOMAS
Child and Adolescent Therapist
Coauthor of *Becoming a Dad:*
A Spiritual, Emotional and Practical Guide

"Knowing and watching Katherine as a gifted teacher at the school my children attend, it's evident that she has a great deal of wisdom and insight. Thankfully, she takes the time to share her gifts with all of us through this book."

STEVEN CURTIS CHAPMAN
Singer/songwriter

"Raising children in the hectic pace of life is hard, but Katherine Koonce brings divine truth about parenting down to earth."

KIM HILL
Worship leader, recording artist, and single mom

"Katherine Koonce directs us to our heavenly Father for the wisdom and purpose we need to parent well. With biblical insights on how to reach a child's heart, she shifts the parental paradigm from our human experience to our one true Parent. Read this book and you'll parent better—and so will your children someday."

DR. RAYMOND C. ORTLUND JR. AND JANI ORTLUND
Authors and senior pastor, Christ Presbyterian Church,
Nashville, Tennessee

"Even though I'm not a parent, the concepts that Katherine illuminates are really helpful for kidless people, too! Her wisdom and practical advice—served up in an engaging and witty style—is pertinent for all of the relationships God calls us into."

LISA HARPER
Author and speaker

"Katherine's ability to state the realities of parenting in a clear and concise manner makes her book meaningful and practical for all parents. Her teaching has touched many lives, and this book will allow many more to benefit from her wisdom."

SUSAN SIMPSON
Homeschool materials publisher,
Common Sense Press

PARENTING *the way* GOD PARENTS

PARENTING
the way GOD
PARENTS

Refusing to Recycle Your Parents' Mistakes

KATHERINE KOONCE

Multnomah Publishers® *Sisters, Oregon*

PARENTING THE WAY GOD PARENTS
published by Multnomah Publishers, Inc.
Published in association with the literary agency of Mark Sweeney
& Associates, 28540 Altessa Way, Suite 201, Bonita Springs, FL 34135
© 2006 by Katherine Koonce
International Standard Book Number: 1-59052-573-6

Cover design by The DesignWorks Group, Inc.
Interior design and typeset by Katherine Lloyd, The DESK

Unless otherwise indicated, Scripture quotations are from:
The Holy Bible, New International Version © 1973, 1984 by International Bible
Society, used by permission of Zondervan Publishing House

Other Scripture quotations are from:
The Message by Eugene H. Peterson, Copyright © 1993, 1994, 1995, 1996, 2000.
Used by permission of NavPress Publishing Group. All rights reserved.

Multnomah is a trademark of Multnomah Publishers, Inc.,
and is registered in the U.S. Patent and Trademark Office.
The colophon is a trademark of Multnomah Publishers, Inc.

Printed in the United States of America

For information:
MULTNOMAH PUBLISHERS, INC.
601 NORTH LARCH STREET • SISTERS, OREGON 97759

Library of Congress Cataloging-in-Publication Data

Koonce, Katherine.
Parenting the way God parents : refusing to recycle your parents' mistakes /
Katherine Koonce.
    p. cm.
Includes bibliographical references.
ISBN 1-59052-573-6
1. Child rearing--Religious aspects--Christianity. 2. Parenting--Religious aspects--
Christianity. I. Title.
BV4529.K67 2006
248.8'45--dc22
                                                                2005025586
06 07 08 09 10 11 12 13 14 — 10 9 8 7 6 5 4 3 2 1 0

To the one who partners with me daily
in this odyssey we call parenting—
to the wisest man I know.

CONTENTS

Introduction 11

Chapter 1   The Family Tree 19

Chapter 2   A Life of Excellence 35

Chapter 3   Drawing the Boundary Lines 51

Chapter 4   Life in Abundance 69

Chapter 5   The Lessons of Choice 85

Chapter 6   Surprised by Anger 103

Chapter 7   With My Whole Heart 119

Chapter 8   Growing Through Disappointment 135

Chapter 9   The Opportunity of a Lifetime 151

Chapter 10 The Entitlement Trap 165

Chapter 11 The Lost Art of Patience 181

Chapter 12 Merciful Uncertainty 197

Conclusion 211

Recommended Resources 215

INTRODUCTION

I don't know you. I don't know anything about your past, your lifestyle, your level of income, your likes and dislikes. I have no idea what aspirations and dreams you have, what hopes you hold for the future, what plans you're making. But I know you are a fellow parent, and this tells me much about you.

This tells me that you have been charged with the weighty task of raising your children, and that you want to do this well. What's more, I know that God your Father has called you to the task, and that He will equip you for it if you will simply learn from Him as you go. I expect that you, like me, have made many mistakes in your parenting, some of which you bitterly regret. There are days when you can think of nothing you would rather be than a parent to your children and other days when you long to be alone on a beach somewhere, far out of reach of those same children. You've both laughed and cried with your children; you've rejoiced over them and wept over them. You've disciplined them fairly at times and unfairly at other times. I know you sometimes feel adequate for the task and sometimes woefully inadequate. There are times you wish you could stop time and gather your children to you and hold them forever just as they are, and there are times you cannot wait for them to get through the difficult stage they're in. But most of all, I know your Parent, your *Abba*-Father. He alone holds the truth and the wisdom and the purpose you and I need in order to parent well.

> *Your Parent, your Abba Father, alone holds*
> *the truth and the wisdom and the purpose you*
> *and I need in order to parent well.*

At any given time, I could point out some specific difficulty in my own home—arguing siblings, tension between us parents, financial stress, difficulties relating to each other for any number of reasons. Could you say the same about your family? Family stress is not unique to my family, nor is it unique to yours. But even when all we see is stress, if we look with the eyes of Our Father, we can see growth, we see relationships being built, we see a legacy of love being passed from Our Father to us and from us to our children.

To understand our own families, we have to acknowledge God as the creator and sustainer of the family. God designed the family in such a way that our parenting would follow the pattern of His parenting. Throughout history, God has parented His people, been angry with them, forgiven them, taught them to cooperate with one another, reprimanded them, required them to make things right when possible—and He has had to do it over and over and over again. Sound familiar? These are the tasks that are ours when we parent our own children.

Psychologists tell us that without conscious effort, we will parent the way we were parented ourselves. We will recycle the parenting, particularly the mistakes, of our own parents. For lack of another plan, we simply do what was done to us. Sometimes this can be good and right, and it brings back sweet memories of our own childhood. Sometimes it is harsh and confusing, and we are alarmed that our parents' mistakes with us are being recycled and used in our own parenting. Like it or not, parenting the way we were parented—the good, the bad, and the ugly—is exactly what we do when we have no other plan.

So perhaps we need a plan.

Much-needed attention has been given in recent decades to talking with children about life's most dangerous pastimes, such as drug and alcohol abuse, sexual activity outside of marriage, and entertainment choices that tear at the fabric of decency and even common sense. Every family needs to create an atmosphere in which these topics are freely discussed, but it is a shortsighted exercise if more foundational issues are ignored.

Family discussions about such topics as devotion, charity, heritage, and excellence must find their way back into our living rooms. As Kingdom parents, we have to go to deeper places of discussion with our children than simply their outward behavior. Jesus warns against working to make people look good on the outside while neglecting the more important heart issues like patience and faith in the face of uncertainty. His feelings are strong when he rebukes the religious leaders: "Woe to you, teachers of the law and Pharisees, you hypocrites! You are like whitewashed tombs, which look beautiful on the outside but on the inside are full of dead men's bones and everything unclean. In the same way, on the outside you appear to people as righteous but on the inside you are full of hypocrisy and wickedness" (Matthew 23:27–28). Granted, no parent seeks to raise a child to be a "whitewashed tomb," but if all our parenting hours are spent directing, shaping, and controlling outside behavior, we are giving our children the wrong message.

PARENTING AS WE WERE PARENTED

Today we have an abundance of information about children and development, more solid facts than ever about what works and what doesn't. And still we struggle to know what to do and when to do it. With this in mind, it is easier to forgive our own parents for their mistakes and to recognize God's hand in our lives through childhood despite those mistakes.

What was life like at your house when you were growing up? What do you remember about your own childhood, your family life, and your relationship with your parents? Imagine you are walking to the front door of the house where you grew up. You are a child again and your family is as it was when you were a child. Walking up to the front door, you reach for the knob and open the door. What does it look like? What do you find there? More important, what are your feelings as you open the door? Are you excited to be home? Are you fearful of what you might find there? Do you sense a strange mixture of both certainty and confusion?

When I went through this exercise, I was surprised to see the things I saw and to feel the feelings of my childhood once again. My childhood home was scarred by alcoholism and all of the turmoil and confusion that brings. Certainly, for myself and almost everyone, there are difficult parts of our childhood histories as well as good and happy times. Some have many good memories of loving and caring parents and of carefree childhoods. Most of us can look back as adults and realize that our parents probably did the best they could. Nevertheless, we are often left feeling unprepared for the task of parenting no matter what example we have to draw from. How are we to know how to be good parents if we were not parented perfectly?

While you or I may not have been parented well as children, we are parented well today.

The Scriptures are a story of how beautifully and perfectly God parents His children. We often look to the Scriptures for verses that give explicit instructions for raising our children, but there are few. Yet throughout Scripture we find the purest and most effective way to parent our children, a framework for how we are to relate to our own children. You see, God is the Parent. He has parented His children from the time of Adam to the present with no breaks, vacations, or time-outs. His Word holds for us the keys to disciplining, training, nurturing, loving, and knowing our children. He is the model for our roles as parents, and He is the source of the wisdom, the discipline, and the grace we need daily—hourly—to parent our children well. In short, as our Father, He offers us a legacy of love, of truth, of wisdom—of everything we need to parent well.

> **The Scriptures are a story of how beautifully and perfectly God parents His children.**

How has God parented you recently? Has He shown you areas in which you need to change your behavior? Has He comforted you when life has battered and hurt you? Has He taught you how to set your priorities or how to change your thinking about some area of your life? Has He affirmed your strengths and gifts and reminded you to use them to benefit others? Has He disciplined you by allowing the natural consequences of your behavior to take effect?

God's parenting doesn't stop when we become adults. When we are children, God disciplines us through our parents, teachers, and other authority figures. When we become adults, God parents us directly, giving us our own model of how to parent our children.

Now that it is our turn to parent, we must recognize that the way we were raised has a profound effect on our parenting style. The Bible tells us to honor our mother and father (Exodus 20:12); this applies to us whether they have lived honorably or not. Yet, this is not to say that we must remember only the good in our parents and ignore the rest. Honoring my parents includes recognizing that they were sinful and broken people, just as I am. I remember the joy they brought me and the pain. One does not nullify the other. And now, with children of my own, I still honor my parents even when I choose not to use some of their parenting tactics. In turn, our children will honor us if they learn from our mistakes in a way that makes them better parents to their own children.

Consider this Scripture in which God describes Himself:

> Then the LORD came down in the cloud and stood there with [Moses] and proclaimed his name, the LORD. And he passed in front of Moses, proclaiming, "The LORD, the LORD, the compassionate and gracious God, slow to anger, abounding in love and faithfulness, maintaining love to thousands, and forgiving wicked-

ness, rebellion and sin. Yet he does not leave the guilty unpunished." (Exodus 34:5–7)

God gives us a picture of Himself as a loving, compassionate Parent who speaks the truth and maintains high ideals of right and wrong. He establishes Himself as the authority—*proclaiming His name, the* LORD. He is merciful and kind to His children and treats them graciously. He is not quick to become angry with His children, ever aware of their childish, sinful natures. His heart is bursting with love and faithfulness. He is willing to forgive His wayward children their sin and rebellion, but He also punishes them as part of His loving discipline.

This is only one of many Scripture snapshots of God as our Parent. As we examine them in the pages ahead, I want you to consider the ways you have chosen, whether by conscious choice or by default, to parent the children God has entrusted to you. As you read the Scriptures, you will discern a plan for parenting based not on how you were parented, but rather on how you *are* parented by God Himself.

God uses life's everyday occurrences to teach and train us. Rather than artificially creating "learning experiences" for His children, He uses the windows of opportunity that life affords. In light of this, we will focus our study on themes that are universal to the childhood experience—to the human experience—such as disappointment, making choices, and dealing with uncertainty.

Each chapter will give you practical suggestions, but will also include reminders to prayerfully consider your specific situation. I'm not going to tell you what to do as much as I'm going to challenge you to think and pray, sometimes extensively, based on the new paradigm of parenting the way you are being parented. After all, God Himself has entrusted your children to you, not to me. You can confidently seek His way for your children because He is faithful!

My hopes for you during your reading of this book are simple. First, I pray that you may know the love your Father has for you, His child, and recognize that while we delight in our children on their best days and in their shining moments, God's delight in us is boundless even on our worst days. I hope that you will value your role as a calling of great importance and great fulfillment, an adventure God continuously equips you for. I pray that you will recognize the ways you are recycling your parents' mistakes, your own mistakes, and the mistakes of society as you relate to your children, and that you will have the courage to lay those down. And lastly, I pray that He will reveal to you the beautiful legacy of love He is passing to you and that He intends for you in turn to pass to your children as you raise them in His presence.

Note: None of the examples of children or families used in this book refer to specific people, except those of my own family.

Chapter One

THE FAMILY TREE

My love of richly seasoned food comes from my mother's side of the family. Her father grew up in a strong French Acadian family in southern Louisiana. The family homestead sat across the street from the Mississippi River and had to be moved more than once because "that river has a mind of its own." There was always something spicy and delicious bubbling on the stove. My grandfather always seemed most at home in his kitchen. He studied the art of cooking, contributed to cookbooks, wrote numerous articles about cooking and entertaining, and hosted grand dinner parties regularly. Our family get-togethers, whether formal or informal, were always accented with delicious food, beautifully prepared.

I have especially vivid memories of our holiday dinners. The dining room table, laden with my grandfather's cooking, could stretch to seat twenty-two, and often did as distant relatives came to town. Some of our relatives were a bit eccentric (a few were downright rude), yet we children were expected to be on our best behavior, to practice our best manners, and to pay close attention to the conversation. We were polite and respectful, even to the distant uncle or second cousin who never had a kind word for any of us children. As you can imagine, it seemed unfair at the time, having to be polite no matter what. Now I recognize that it taught me to maintain my best manners even when others do not, a lesson that has served me well in my adult life.

My grandparents subscribed to the old theory that "children should be seen and not heard." This philosophy taught us our place as children within the extended family structure. We learned much about the adult world just by listening quietly to conversations around the table. We were never in the spotlight and were rarely asked to join in the conversation. We were present simply because we were part of the family, and we learned to be gracious to our relatives simply because they were also part of the family.

So it's clear that an appreciation for Cajun cooking and good manners derive from my family heritage. But there's much more than that. I find my family has armed me with the tenacity to persevere in the midst of struggles, a strong work ethic, a love of the written word, and an intense satisfaction in a story well told. Of course, I realize that I am romanticizing my family background and that there is an equally long list of inherited traits that are not so admirable. No doubt the same could be said of anyone.

The Good, the Bad, and the Ugly

I used to cringe when I heard people say how much I reminded them of my father. His influence made much of my childhood tumultuous and emotionally painful. For years I recalled nothing but the harsh and selfish aspects of his personality. I remembered no tender moments or real affection, and very little about him that made me proud. In my memory, he had no redeeming qualities.

As I have aged and had children of my own, I recognize that family life is not so black and white. Yes, there was bad in our family, but there was some good, too, and an awful lot of gray. I am like my father in a lot of ways. I am opinionated and not easily intimidated. Like him, I pull for the underdog every time. I can be brash and careless with the feelings of others if I'm not paying attention. I appreciate humor as he did, and like him, I have little patience with people who have no sense of humor.

My father and grandfather are two of the many contributors to my heritage—the good, the bad, and the ugly of it. I recognize now that heritage not only consists of traditions and cultural practices, but also includes the passing of character traits, of personal preferences, of perspective. More important, I recognize that it is my responsibility to consciously choose which aspects of my family heritage to pass along to my own children.

> *It is my responsibility to consciously choose which aspects of my family heritage to pass along to my own children.*

The families that populate the Scriptures are of the richest variety. In their family stories we find plenty of examples of what to do, and plenty more of what *not* to do. There are accounts of children learning from the mistakes of their parents. In 2 Chronicles we learn that King Uzziah's downfall was his pride (2 Chronicles 26). But his son, Jotham, wisely learns from his father's prideful mistakes and chooses instead to practice respect for God's temple (2 Chronicles 27). Fathers like Isaac bless their children, and others withhold their blessing (Genesis 27). Loyal brothers stand up for each other, and brothers like Joseph's betray each other (Genesis 37). We see God binding together the remnants of broken families, as with Naomi and Ruth (Ruth 1). Even in the lineage of Jesus we find King David, an adulterer as well as a man after God's own heart (1 Samuel 13:14), and Rahab, heroine of the battle for the Promised Land and a…well, a prostitute. It seems that every family is a bag of mixed nuts—of mediocrity and overachievement, of success stories and embarrassments. In a broken and unrighteous world, could this be God's design for the family?

The Bible is clear about this one aspect of our earthly families— they are going to let us down. Guaranteed. God is called a *Father to the fatherless* (Psalm 68:5), and we are told that He *defends the cause of the fatherless* (Deuteronomy 10:18), because there will always be parents who fail their children.

How then should we consider our own family's heritage? Should we pretend that the bad did not exist, or that it was of no consequence? Sometimes this is my tendency. Yet, there are aspects of my heritage that truly bring me pain, as much as I would like to deny it. Like many of you, I live daily with child-hood scars, and consequently I sometimes struggle with fears and insecurities about my own parenting.

On the other hand, it may be tempting for us to blame any and all current difficulties on our upbringing. Certainly, pain inflicted by one's family cuts deeper than any other; however, to dwell in that pain and deny God's ability to heal isn't the answer either. So, what place should these memories have in my life, in my heart? Answering this question is of great importance to parents, because it will affect not only our lives but those of our children.

A Heritage of Sin

Family customs, holiday traditions, old family stories—these are not all that we pass from generation to generation. Often some of the same sins that plagued our parents and grandparents influence us, too. This can be as minor as a tendency to stretch the truth when telling a story or as debilitating as alcoholism or abuse. Every family is made up of human beings who struggle with sin.

It is a sad aspect of human nature that growing up in the midst of sinful behavior often blinds us to its presence. We don't recognize it because we're so used to it. An abused child may grow up to believe that hitting someone is a valid way to communicate a point, or he may even believe that he deserves the abuse. The child of a raging parent grows up to believe that out-of-control behavior is normal and acceptable, and he will likely imitate that behavior as an adult. It is difficult for children in a family that lives from crisis to crisis to recognize stability when they see it. Sinful attitudes such as prejudice, pride, and resentment can be particularly insidious. We need to examine ourselves fearlessly for sin that has passed to us from previous generations.

Of course, no one wants to pass generational sin on to his children. But simply not wanting to is not enough. We have to take a more active role. Just as God our Father is a shield and protector to us (Psalm 28:7), we must shield our children, praying against specific generational sin and looking honestly at ourselves for signs of its influence. If we are willing to look openly and honestly at ourselves, we will be better prepared to spot problems as they arise in our family. Since we cannot change a problem that we refuse to acknowledge as a problem, it is especially important to ask God to show us the ways we are passing negative aspects of our earthly heritage on to our children. This is part of the loving way He parents us, showing us, in due time, those areas in which we need to change and grow.

It is especially important to ask God to show us the ways we are passing negative aspects of our earthly heritage on to our children.

Choosing What to Pass Along

It can be difficult to think about which aspects of my childhood family I want to pass along to my children. Even though I may choose to parent the way I am parented rather than the way I was parented, my earthly heritage is still a part of who I am.

Rather than simply passing along traditions, beliefs, and ideals just as they came to me, and rather than rejecting them altogether, I have a third option. I can consider them in light of the children God has given me. For example, in my childhood family, books were very important. My grandmother was a librarian; my grandfather was a writer. My parents both read voraciously, and we were encouraged to do the same. When my other grandmother from Texas came to visit, she always brought a suitcase full of books. We fondly remember one visit in which she arrived with her suitcase full of books, but had forgotten to pack another suitcase of clothes!

The love of reading instilled by my family has greatly enhanced my faith over the years, as I have so naturally loved to read God's Word. I want to pass along to my children this same love of reading and learning so that, along with simply enjoying a good read, they will also study and search the Scriptures in their own walks with God. This is one way that, as God parents me, He redeems and uses aspects of my earthly heritage to strengthen and deepen my faith in Him. I trust that He will do the same for my children as they consider which aspects of our family God would have them pass along to their children.

I encourage you to consider those difficulties, which you recognize from your family of origin, that have surfaced in your current family. It's important to pinpoint them, to write them down, and to pray regularly about them, committing them to the Lord. This is a true faith-walk, because most everything in our experience leads us to feel fatalistic about generational struggles. We think, "My grandmother struggled with this, and my mother struggled with it, so I guess I'll struggle with it, too." No! God is bigger than this; He's bigger than your family's baggage. If you let Him, He will not only heal the wounds caused by those struggles, He will also free you from them and even use them to equip you to help others to be free from theirs. What a beautiful way for God to show you how well He parents you.

A FAMILY VISION

My husband's grandmother had theories about the families she grew up with. The Greenfields were always stingy. All the Bartons were generous to a fault. You had to take what any Hampton said with a grain of salt. As far as she was concerned, family traits were part of family heritage and were unlikely to change. She put into words what we all sense, that one's background influences his mannerisms and preferences. It is less clear, however, how much more our family heritage touches the vision of the family we hope to become.

The influence of our family heritage extends beyond the present and into the future, affecting our perspective on life and therefore the future we imagine. *Here too, we are not bound by our earthly heritage.* Embracing the heritage of our heavenly Father and the vision He holds for our family, we begin to discover a vision for our family's future that is in line with our heavenly birthright.

> *Embracing the heritage of our heavenly*
> *Father and the vision He holds for our family,*
> *we begin to discover a vision for our family's future*
> *that is in line with our heavenly birthright.*

We often do not recognize that we have been living without vision for our families until something occurs that shows us how far off we are. For example, I may not recognize that my children are spending too much time in front of the television until I notice they cannot form complete sentences at the dinner table. Likewise, it may not be until my child comes home with a string of bad grades that I realize we've not made homework a priority. On a more serious note, it may take a phone call from the authorities to confront us with the reality that our child is involved in something dangerous. Times like these shock us into recognizing the need to examine our lives and reprioritize.

As we seek God's vision for our own family, we can observe how God communicated His plans for His children in the past. One of the earliest family visions was the one God passed down to Abraham, who at the time was named Abram. God told this seventy-five-year-old, childless man that he would become the father of a great nation and that his descendants would out-number the very stars. Not only would God's blessing rest on Abram's family, but it would also extend through them to fall on many others for many generations to come. In fact, God said, "All peoples on earth will be blessed through you" (Genesis 12:3). What a vision!

Leaving the Familiar Behind

But let's rewind the conversation God had with Abram a bit. Just before revealing this vision, God asked Abram to leave his country, his relatives, his father's homestead, and go to a land he had never even heard of. This was a significant part of God's plan for Abram, and it is an equally significant part of His plan for our families. He wants us to leave the things that are familiar—the way things have always been—and to go out in faith, building a family of His design. It's easy to build a family of our own design, but God invites us to throw off what we think we know and open ourselves up to His vision for our families. Just as God challenged Abram to trust in His plan, He calls us to trust Him wholeheartedly with our families.

God may ask us to leave behind some of the comfortable

and familiar ways of child rearing that we grew up with. He has asked me, for instance, to leave behind the practice of parenting in anger and using sarcasm with my children. While my natural response is to react defensively when I'm questioned, He has asked me to leave that behind as well. When I find myself running back to pick up some of those discarded ways, my Father gently but clearly asks me to put them back down again. Perhaps He has asked you to leave behind some of the parenting traits you have become comfortable with. Is He asking you to let go of unfair expectations of your children, or of a parenting style that is too permissive? Has He asked you to leave behind some of the activities that take you away from home so you have enough time for your family? Whatever your Father has asked you to discard in your journey with Him, be assured that He will more than replace it with joy and peace that only He can give.

When God asked Abram to leave everything, one of the things he left was idol worship. Even though I've never melted down my jewelry and fashioned a gold cow, I do have idols that I am tempted to worship, and I'll bet you do, too. Many of them are centered on my children. As soon as we become parents, we begin forming hopes and dreams for our children. We make plans for their limitless success and their universal acclaim. We want them to have opportunities we didn't have, to experience success beyond anything in our experience. But we must remember that our best hopes and dreams for our children pale in comparison to those God has for them. We may actually be clinging to a vision for our family that is counter to God's vision. When this is the case, that vision becomes an idol.

The only way we will be unleashed as a family is to lay down those preconceived notions, those plans we've held so tightly, those idols, and become fully open to what God has for us.

> *Our best hopes and dreams for*
> *our children pale in comparison to*
> *those God has for them.*

FAMILY VALUES

While we ask God to reveal His intentions for our families, we also seek to discover those godly values that should drive our thinking and our behavior as a family. Our Father gives us lots of direction in the Bible about the things He thinks are important in life. Here are just a few. You might want to look them up and read them aloud as a family.

- Clothe yourselves with compassion, kindness, humility, gentleness and patience. (Colossians 3:12–14)
- Children, obey your parents in everything. (Colossians 3:20)
- Don't do anything out of selfish ambition or vain conceit. (Philippians 2:3)
- Work wholeheartedly, as if you were serving the Lord. (Ephesians 6:7)
- Be a cheerful giver. (2 Corinthians 9:7)
- Do justice, love mercy, and walk humbly with your God. (Micah 6:8)

While every verse of Scripture has the potential to affect every Christian, it is important to seek out verses that hold special significance in your family.

Over the years I have watched with interest as God has established different families in our church to serve different purposes. Each family has sought to be faithful and to live by the teachings of the Bible, but they are anything but cookie-cutter duplicates. One family in our church brings great encouragement to others whenever it is needed. Another family, blessed with financial resources, gives generously to others. I believe our own family has a distinct purpose: to serve others and to help those in need. The distinctives of a family—those attributes that define it uniquely—are a part of the heritage we seek to communicate to our children.

If I spent a week in your home and watched your family members interact with each other, what would I be able to tell about your values and beliefs? I know that in our home, what we value is not always obvious from the way we spend our time. We must not forget to regularly talk through our family's values, reminding our children and ourselves what we believe is important, and arranging our lives accordingly.

> *We must not forget to regularly talk through our family's values, reminding our children and ourselves what we believe is important, and arranging our lives accordingly.*

As an exercise to get the family talking along these lines, make a list of the ten most important values you want to com-

municate to your children. Do you want to encourage thrifti-
ness? How about kindness to others? Are studying and learning
important to you? What about compassion, authenticity, and
faithfulness? Certainly all of us want to emphasize these and a
hundred other traits in our children. But try to prayerfully narrow it down to the top ten or so for your family. Consider as
well what sets your family apart from others. What would you
say were the defining characteristics of your family? Once
you've started the ball rolling in discussions like these, it will be
easier for you to discover God's unique vision for your family.

A Godly Heritage

As we build for our families a heritage that is strong and right,
we must consider not only those characteristics we have inherited from our families of origin, but also those we have
inherited from our heavenly Father. The traits, gifts, and apti-
tudes we have received from God our Father are part of the
heavenly heritage we want to pass along to future generations.

God teaches us to make a clear distinction between our
earthly heritage and our godly heritage. For instance, all Abram
wanted was to have a son to carry on the family name. The
chances of this happening were not good, and in his old age
Abram had resigned himself to his place at the end of his family
line. But God gave Abram a godly heritage. He changed Abram's
name to Abraham as a symbol of His intervention, replacing his
earthly heritage with a godly one. In the same way, Jacob's
scheming and deceitful ways were traded for a new heritage
when he wrestled with God. Jacob's name was changed to
Israel as a sign of God's intervention (Genesis 3:24–30). The

apostle Paul's name was changed from Saul when he renounced his earthly heritage and chose instead to pass along God's heritage to unbelievers worldwide (Acts 9).

There is a definite moment in the life of each believer—just as there was in Abraham's, Jacob's, and Paul's lives—in which he chooses to be a part of God's family. No matter what our age, we let go of our hold on this world. We let go of our earthy heritage as the authority over how we are to think, to feel, and to live. We let God create a new heritage in us. As parents, we are charged with passing this new godly heritage along to our children.

Consider This...

- What aspects of your earthly family heritage—beliefs, traditions, customs—do you believe God would have you pass along to your children? Are there aspects of your heritage you are not comfortable passing to your children? Why?

- Is it possible that there is a generational sin that has been passed on in your family? What is that sin—or, as in my case, those sins?

- What is it about your family that sets it apart from others? What would you say were the defining characteristics of your family?

- How has God uniquely equipped your family for ministry? What opportunities for ministry to others has God presented to your family in recent years?

Chapter Two

A LIFE
OF EXCELLENCE

I got into my fair share of trouble growing up. I remember many times I let my siblings or my friends tell me how to live. My brother, in particular, was a strong influence on me. Randy was one year older and never at a loss for ideas—most of which led to our getting into trouble. He questioned authority at every turn and encouraged me to do so as well. Even though his schemes were far-fetched, I usually went along with them.

We went to a Catholic school, and the Sisters who taught us were always suspect in my brother's eyes. While in the fourth grade, Randy asked one of the nuns what would happen if he stole a Bible. This was typical Randy-style questioning. I'm sure he embellished her response, but he told me that the Sister said he would go straight to hell—right there on the spot, no questions asked. Naturally, he had to try it, and I would be his witness.

Intrigued at the prospect of seeing someone go straight to hell, I hopped on my banana-seat bicycle and followed Randy to the nearby TG&Y store. We entered the store nonchalantly, looking here and there at different items. Randy spotted the

Bibles and motioned for me to come over. He was going to pocket the Bible and I would watch to see what happened. If he disappeared, I could assume the nun was right after all.

Needless to say, Randy did not go straight to hell, and as he left the store with the stolen Bible, he thought himself vindicated. I'm not sure what ever happened to that Bible, but I came away with the understanding that I needed to be careful about choosing who to follow in life. And it was clear that Randy was not the best choice.

As spiritual children we are wise to look to our Father as our model for excellence, for right living, and for worthy pursuits, but our tendency is to look to each other, our siblings in God's family. We can easily lead each other astray unless at least one of us is looking to the Father in our pursuit of excellence.

Excellence Defined

While the concept of excellence is difficult to characterize, we often define it as a standard of very high quality. But this definition falls short of God's intentions for us. There are endless forms of excellence, and endless ways to measure it. We might measure professional excellence in a career by the size of one's paycheck. We could measure excellence in a sport by the number of titles won or records set. We often measure excellence in school by the grades a student receives. While these may all be appropriate, they are far from complete. How does one measure the excellence of a Mother Teresa, a William Shakespeare, or a Martin Luther King Jr.?

There was a time when the apostle Paul recognized himself to be excellent in the eyes of his political and religious community, but he later learned that this label was utterly devoid of value. He took great pride in his name, his upbringing, his education, and his professional status, until the Damascus road where God revealed to him a different standard. Paul's Father was gracious and merciful enough to teach him about real excellence.

It is tempting to believe that people who are considered excellent by this world's standards are also excellent by God's standards. Just as my brother was not the one to help me understand how to live, we must not look to each other in this world for the standards of excellent living. A six-figure income, children who do well in school, expensive cars, and positions of authority in the community or even church do not necessarily indicate excellence according to God's standards. We must never give our children cause to believe it does.

It is tempting to believe that people who are considered excellent by this world's standards are also excellent by God's standards.

EXCELLENCE REDEFINED

It is inadequate to say that God our Parent is an excellent parent, an excellent Creator, an excellent God. He is excellence. Excellence is in every aspect of His being. His name is majestic (Psalm 8:1), His love is priceless (Psalm 36:7), His greatness surpasses all others (Psalm 150:2), His deeds are glorious (Isaiah 12:5), His counsel is wonderful and His wisdom magnificent (Isaiah 28:29), His power is complete (2 Corinthians 12:9), His will is good, pleasing, and perfect

(Romans 12:2), His gifts are good (James 1:17), and His promises are excellent (2 Peter 1:4).

There is no part of God our Father that is not excellent, including those dark and mysterious places we could never fathom in our mortal states. He moves in ways we don't understand and sometimes fear. But we can be sure that sovereignty and majesty, power and infinite wisdom lie behind His works, because He is excellent.

Because of His excellence, He intends for His children to live lives of excellence as well. In Matthew 5:48, Jesus speaks the great challenge to us believers: "Be perfect, therefore, as your heavenly Father is perfect." This verse has always concerned me. There's no one on the planet who would enjoy being perfect more than I, but I cannot attain it no matter how hard I try (and I've tried!). This verse speaks not only of perfection as God's standard—which is why we need a Savior—but it also illustrates a dimension of the Father–child relationship. God wants us to look to Him for our standard of right living, just as we want our children to look to us rather than to their friends or siblings.

If we're going to look to God our Father as the model for excellence, we need a new definition of the word, one that aligns us with our majestic, priceless, surpassing, glorious, wonderful, magnificent, perfect, and pleasing Father.

To live excellently is to value what God values.

To live excellently is to value what God values.

And what *does* God value? God our Father values people; He values us. He values the relationships we have with one another.

He values the hearts and minds of every person He created. He esteems our praise, our obedience, and our submission to His design for our lives. He urges us to pursue excellence on His terms, not ours. He values the comfort, grace, and mercy we offer one another. He values faithfulness and beauty, wisdom and purity. The Sermon on the Mount reveals that He attributes worth to those who are poor in spirit, those who mourn, and those who are meek. He puts high value on those who hunger and thirst for righteousness. He loves those who show mercy, are pure in heart, and seek peace. He treasures those who are persecuted because of Him (Matthew 5:3–10). These things that God values stand in stark contrast to what the world values. We must make that contrast clear to our children just as God makes it clear to us.

To work at a task excellently is to "work at it with all your heart, as working for the Lord" (Colossians 3:23), so it is important that we make this clear to our children. We want them to do their best, not for us but for their real Parent. We want their confidence to be not in themselves but in God, knowing that He holds the resources needed to live excellently. We want them to be confident in the inheritance they will receive from God and not simply in the praise and compensation they may or may not receive from people. In short, we want them to keep ever aware that they are doing their best for their God and not for us.

TEACHING EXCELLENTLY

Studying God's blueprint for excellence—His Word—we note a marked change in God's parenting style between the two Testaments. In the Old Testament, Israel was under the Law,

God's wise and strong boundaries for living. The Old Testament Law had a flavor of "you shall not" to it. It communicated more about what to keep away from than what to strive toward. The New Testament, the fulfillment of the Old Testament Law, has more of a "you shall" flavor. Our rebirth in Christ takes us from the Old Testament "keep away from sin" to the New Testament "pursue godly excellence."

God is still just as intent on our keeping away from sin as He was during Old Testament times, and we can learn from the wise parenting techniques He uses. He knows that we cannot act in sin and in righteousness at the same time. It's impossible. By encouraging righteousness, living with excellence, He displaces our tendency to sin. So if we are counting others better than ourselves, then we are not being prideful. If we are practicing patience, then we are not being impatient. If we are acting in faith, then we are not being unfaithful.

This is an approach we can apply at home. As we raise our children we certainly want to dissuade them from sinful behavior, but the atmosphere of our homes needs to reflect God's style of parenting and to encourage the children to excellence. In other words, tell them what *to* do more than you tell them what *not* to do.

We can teach a child not to be rude at the table by teaching him how to be polite at the table. A child cannot be polite and rude at the same time. We correct a child for being bossy and rude to his little sister when we instruct him to have a respectful tone of voice when speaking to her. Obviously there are times when you have to tell a child what not to do—don't stick your finger in a light socket, don't play in the street, don't do drugs—but the overall flavor of our parenting can parallel God's, which encourages us toward excellence.

Encouraging Excellence

It is human nature that, when our efforts in any endeavor go unnoticed and unappreciated, we lose the motivation to pursue excellence; when we are esteemed or appreciated in an area of competence, we seek to excel all the more. In America, for instance, the teaching profession is not held in the esteem that it deserves. We see evidence of this in the low salaries, the inadequate support, and the open disrespect teachers face daily in our country. This was made all the more clear to me on a recent trip to China.

Our church sent fifty educators to a city called Yantai to work with Chinese teachers of English. As part of the planning team, I helped to develop the curriculum we would use and also served as a lead teacher while there. The few hundred Chinese teachers we were told to expect grew to about seven hundred as word spread among government officials that teachers were coming from America to teach English. The people of China are eager to learn English as a way to enhance their professional status.

A ramshackle bus carried us from our hotel on the Yellow Sea to the Number One Middle School, so named because it was considered the city's best school facility. When we pulled up to the front gate, we saw hundreds of people seated on the ground, waiting for us to arrive. Some were teachers and school administrators, others were high-ranking government officials, but all were eager to learn from us.

Everyone quieted immediately upon our arrival. As we got off of the bus, the people rose in unison and parted, almost ceremoniously, to open a path through their ranks to the school. We felt immensely valued, part of a highly esteemed profession.

After being welcomed with such dignity, our motivation skyrocketed! We were thrilled to do an excellent job teaching these eager students. Our presentations were more animated; there was more energy in our lectures. We gladly gave our all to these students, knowing that our efforts were appreciated and respected.

What brings out excellence within you—in performance, in attitude, in character? For some, it's being around people who hold excellence in high regard. For others, it's the encouragement of loved ones or colleagues who believe in them. We generally strive for excellence when we think it is worthwhile and when we think we can attain it. I am not the least bit hopeful of excelling in cross-country skiing or in mountain climbing, because I know that I cannot attain excellence, or even competence, in these areas. However, I have enjoyed success in other areas in the past, and it is reasonable to believe I can excel in them. So it is with our children. Confidence breeds confidence. Excellence breeds excellence.

Our children will pursue excellence when they feel competent enough to try. Competence grows from instruction and practice and encouragement. Feeling competent and at the same time being encouraged by a role model sets the stage for a child to pursue excellence. A sports figure is an obvious example of a role model. One Nike commercial's poignant and only words were "I wanna be like Mike," showing the extraordinary influence that Michael Jordan had on countless young people. But a sports figure lacks one ingredient essential for a true role model—a personal relationship with the child. In relationship with a trusted and respected adult, a child learns to value the excellent things in life. A dedicated teacher may inspire a student to academic excellence. A teenager's role model is often a youth pastor who inspires a deeper, more meaningful life of faith. A neighbor, a parent, a grandparent, a big brother or sister— any adult who encourages a child can be a role model for excellence. Children need role models who define excellence as God defines it.

Our children will pursue excellence
when they feel competent enough to try.

THE PERFECTIONISM PIT

Before going further, we need to make an important distinction between excellence and perfection. While it is possible to reach excellence in a given task or pursuit, it is not possible to reach perfection. When we lead children to believe that perfection is their goal, we guarantee that they will fail. Perfection is like north: You can head north but you will never reach north. North is a direction, not a destination. In the same way, you can work toward perfection, but you will never attain perfection. What's more, children who expect perfection of themselves, or believe their parents expect it of them, will eventually stop trying to measure up, because no one can ever measure up to such a standard. This expectation invariably leads to underachievement. Perfectionist children often avoid trying new things or pursuing anything with a lot of energy. Why bother? If the only standard is perfection, they are destined to fail.

There are several ways to help children understand the difference between perfectionism and excellence. If a person is pursuing excellence in something—say, a sport—then mistakes are just a part of the process of becoming good at that sport. In fact, mistakes are important because they can be analyzed and used to improve performance. On the other hand, if a person feels that perfection is the standard, then mistakes are threatening. One way to know if your child might be struggling with perfectionism is to note if he vehemently denies or hides his mistakes.

Another indicator that a child might be struggling with perfectionism is how difficult he finds it to take healthy risks and stretch himself. When a child who wants to be perfect encounters a new or challenging task, he will often avoid trying it because he expects to do poorly at the outset. No child can master everything the first time, but we want him to try new things, to test the waters, to see what he can do. Healthy, growing children are able to take healthy risks. But perfectionist children will underachieve because they won't try an honors class if they think they might not get an A, or they won't go out for that sport if they think they might not be on the starting team.

How to Exasperate a Child

God does not exasperate us with expectations that are unreasonable, and He tells us not to exasperate our children (Ephesians 6:4; Colossians 3:21). Unfortunately, it is fairly easy to exasperate a child. We frustrate our children when our standards are so high that we are never pleased, never satisfied. We exasperate them when all their mistakes are met with correction, while few of their right choices are met with praise. We do not inspire excellence with an "I told you so" attitude. We also discourage them when we simply expect excellence without encouraging and training them toward excellence.

God does not exasperate us with expectations that are unreasonable, and He tells us not to exasperate our children.

Children mature in stages. We have to keep a watchful eye on each of our children to understand not only the developmental stage they are in but also how their unique personalities are reflected within that stage. Children are exasperated when we expect more of them than they are able to do. Knowing our children well includes understanding their development. We pray for the discernment to use this information in setting reasonable expectations of them.

I have often wondered how God decides that one of His children is ready to take on a challenging task. How did God know that Moses was ready to go into Egypt and demand freedom for the Israelite slaves? What told Him that the time was right for David to fight Goliath? What was it about Peter that made Him think this man could fill the role of an apostle? How does God our Parent know that you or I are ready to take on a challenge of His choosing? He pays attention to us; He understands our development (1 Samuel 16:7). That is, God knows when His children are ready because God knows His children.

As we pay attention to our children—to their development and to their individuality—we understand them more fully and so can be wiser about our expectations of them. We will know if our expectations are reasonable or not. In communicating them to our children, we offer generous encouragement by telling them clearly what we expect and also that we know they are capable. We stay away from vague comments such as "I know you can do it" and instead give praise that is specific: "With your great skills at organization, I know you'll be able to make this work." Define a range of acceptable performance. If we're talking about grades, for instance, we might set the range of acceptability between a low B and mid-level A. For other children, or for different school situations, the range may need to be a bit lower. Whatever the range, leave a little room at the top for the child to wow us with better-than-required work. Never tell a child that you expect all As or even As and Bs, because then even if he makes a 99 on a test, he's still done no better than was expected. Rather, if his range is low B to mid A and he earns a 99, then he has performed above expectation, and it's time to dole out some praise!

What should we do if our child consistently falls short of our expectations? The natural response is to assume that his abilities or his motivation are not strong enough. However, many factors have the potential to interfere with a child's ability to succeed in a given area. Learning difficulties, problems with attention and concentration, a classroom environment that is not conducive to his learning style, an underdeveloped work ethic, physical limitations, or social pressures are just a few reasons children might not reach excellence in school, in sports, or in any arena. If a child has experienced failure time and time again, he will be much less likely to work with energy and gusto. Difficult experiences in life cause some children to underachieve, even when the experiences are unrelated to the task at hand. Some children have so little confidence in their abilities that even when their abilities are solid, they don't even try.

> *Some children have so little confidence*
> *in their abilities that even when their*
> *abilities are solid, they don't even try.*

THE MARBLE GIVERS

Failure can be devastating to a child who has no mechanisms in place to help him bounce back from it. Working with a discouraged child to encourage him toward excellence is a slow and steady process that begins with—marbles. (Stay with me through this analogy.) When good things happen to a child— he gets a good grade, she gets a compliment from her dad, his team wins the baseball game—they get the emotional equivalent of marbles. A marble for a right answer in class. Another marble for sitting at lunch with the cool kids. Still another marble for being late to class and not getting caught. Some children have loads of marbles. Others have very few, because they are taken away one by one every time they fail a test or don't get picked for a team or don't get invited to a party. When it comes to taking a risk in childhood—such as attempting to answer the teacher's question or asking a friend over to play— you run the risk of losing marbles if you get the answer wrong or if your friend doesn't want to play with you.

If you are a child with an emotional backpack full of

marbles, then you can afford to lose a few. So you take risks without even thinking about it. But if you are a kid who is down to only two marbles, are you going to raise your hand to answer a question in class? No way! You might lose your last two marbles! So you keep your hand down, even if you know the answer, protecting yourself while passing up yet another opportunity to pursue excellence.

So what is our job as parents? We are marble givers. We are to watch our children so we can discern their capabilities and then meet them there with praise and admiration. We give marbles—lots of them—for their efforts and their risk taking. Just as God our Father is extravagant with His blessings on us, we make extravagant statements such as "I'm impressed! How did you learn to do that?" and "Way to go! You stuck it out and finished. You've got great stamina." We need to remember that we give kids the most marbles when we simply spend time with them, taking interest in them and talking to them about their interests. And in turn, that child is better equipped to begin his own pursuit of excellence.

Consider This...

- What does it mean to be excellent? What are some ways we can tell that someone has done something excellently? Ask your children these questions to get a better feel for their perspective on excellence.

- Who has God put in your life to encourage you to pursue excellence in your parenting? How do they encourage you?

- Is there anything you can think of that someone does to try to encourage you, but that really does not encourage you at all? Now, what might you be doing to try to encourage your children toward excellence that might instead be discouraging to them?

- Do you have a child who struggles with perfectionism? What makes you think so? What can you do to help him distinguish between the pursuit of excellence and debilitating perfectionism?

- Do you have a child who needs some more marbles of encouragement? How can you give those marbles in an honest and genuine way?

Chapter Three

DRAWING THE
BOUNDARY LINES

A recent TV documentary described a research study about what happens to children's behavior when there are no adults present and no rules. The children—about twenty of them—were left in a playroom with some hidden cameras. To make matters even more interesting, the researchers placed several forbidden objects in the room, such as a gun (unloaded of course) and other dangerous no-no's. Well, I don't know how much the researchers spent on this study, but they could have saved a lot of time and money had they just asked you or me or any other parent.

The behavior in that little room showed what happens daily, hourly, across the country when children are left to their own devices. It's a cross between *Lord of the Flies* and Armageddon. In the research study, every child's natural behavior was exaggerated. The quiet children got quieter and more withdrawn. The active children got hyperactive. The bossy children got even bossier. The stronger personalities took over, and some began to victimize those with weaker personalities. What was most interesting to me, however, was that the children's parents had been asked to predict how their children would behave; without exception, after viewing the film, each parent was appalled to see how their little darlings handled themselves. Even though they foresaw the general chaos that occurred, every parent had expected his child to have better self-control, better personal boundaries.

Why do children behave this way when they think no one is watching? Why do adults, for that matter? The researchers concluded that it was because of our innate "animal instincts." God has another term for that—our sinful nature. Because we are imperfect beings, we need boundaries to help us know where we stand, to limit our selfish instincts, and to protect both others and ourselves.

> *Because we are imperfect beings,*
> *we need boundaries to help us know where*
> *we stand, to limit our selfish instincts, and to*
> *protect both others and ourselves.*

THE BEAUTY OF BOUNDARIES

Drs. Henry Cloud and John Townsend coined this use of the term *boundaries* in their series of books on this subject. A personal boundary, according to Cloud and Townsend, is a predetermined limit regarding how you will behave in certain situations, what you will tolerate in others, and how you will allow other people's behavior to affect you. You might have a personal boundary, for example, that says you will not overcommit yourself to activities outside the home. A behavioral boundary, on the other hand, has to do with the behavior of others over whom you have authority. These are predetermined limits that show the line between allowed behavior and disallowed behavior. Companies establish behavioral boundaries in the form of policies about expected employee conduct, employer responsibility, and company response to misbehavior. In the home, we establish boundaries when we set consequences for certain behaviors, when we allow or disallow privileges, and when we assign responsibilities to the children. This all sounds simple enough in theory, but in practice things get a little dicey.

Trouble comes for everyone involved when the boundaries we set in our homes are unclear or subject to change without notice. In these situations our children are kept guessing as to what is expected of them. If I tell my children that burping aloud is a disgusting habit and I won't allow it at the table, but then I do allow it when it's funny or when I'm in a good mood or when my children are being particularly adorable, then my boundaries on that subject become fuzzy, and my children will be confused.

God, our Father, is always very clear about the boundaries He sets for His children.

God, our Father, is always very clear about the boundaries He sets for His children. Here are a few:

- Be imitators of God. (Ephesians 5:1)
- Love your neighbor as yourself. (Matthew 19:19)

- Speak the truth in love. (Ephesians 4:15)
- Love not just with words but also with actions and in truth. (1 John 3:18)
- Honor your father and mother. (Exodus 20:12)

These may look initially like rules, but look closer. The boundaries set by God cannot be kept unless one's heart is pure and committed to living by faith. God is not interested in our simply keeping the rules but then harboring self-righteousness, unforgiveness, and selfishness in our hearts. Look back at that list of "rules" above. Could you possibly stay within those boundaries if your heart wasn't completely devoted to God?

And God knows we will occasionally wander out of the boundary lines, as any child does, and when we do, we reap the consequences. These consequences may come in the form of broken relationships, unfulfilled potential, and having to work to make things right again. When God sets a boundary, He enforces it.

The importance of teaching a child this concept of sowing and reaping—of staying within the bounds or having to reap the consequences—cannot be overstated. In setting and keeping boundaries, in administering consequences when we say we're going to, we are teaching more than just table manners or respect for the property of others. We are modeling a profound and often-missed truth, established by God our Father from the beginning of time—it is ridiculous to sow one thing and expect to reap another.

PERSONAL BOUNDARIES

One type of boundary is the personal boundary, which is established by the person who holds it. Throughout Scripture, God sets His personal boundaries to communicate to us what we can expect of Him, how He's going to act, and how He will respond to our behavior. We do the same for our children. For example, you may establish a boundary that says, "I'm not going to help you with your homework after nine o'clock," or "I'm not going to bring something to school you've accidentally left at home." Personal boundaries communicate to the people around you what they can expect from you in certain areas. If your children know that punctuality is important to you, then they will more likely get ready on time so as not to miss their ride. When a discussion with your child or teenager begins to deteriorate into an argument, you may exercise a personal boundary by going into another room for a cooling-off period. In doing so, you establish that you're not going to argue in anger with your child. The key to establishing personal boundaries is to do so ahead of time, not in the heat of the moment. This is important to your children, because they need to know what they can expect from you. Your children need for you to be consistent. If you set a boundary, then you must do your best to keep it.

> *Your children need for you to be consistent.*
> *If you set a boundary, then you must*
> *do your best to keep it.*

Remember, personal boundaries are about you—your behavior, your reactions, and your decisions. Your children need to see that you have personal boundaries, that you are not merely a short-order cook, a maid, a chauffeur. When we have no personal boundaries, we teach and even encourage disrespect in our children. While no parent sets out to be disrespected, the family naturally deteriorates into disrespect for one another when the individuals have no boundaries. Perhaps you grew up in a home in which one parent had no personal boundaries or a parent did not respect your boundaries. It will be all the more important for you to carefully and prayerfully consider your own boundaries.

BEHAVIORAL BOUNDARIES

Another important type of boundary is the behavioral boundary. This is a limit we set as parents to confine our children's behavior. Throughout the Old and New Testaments, God has set boundaries for His children's behavior. In Leviticus, there were laws about what they could eat, how they should work, and when they should rest. These boundaries were established for their well-being. Other laws reflect God's values regarding matters of the heart. Forgive each other (Colossians 3:13). Don't harbor covetousness in your heart (Exodus 20:17). Be kind and compassionate (Colossians 3:12). Likewise, we need to consider both our children's safety and our family values when we set boundaries.

In starting a list of behavioral boundaries for your home, first choose the most important behaviors. I often encourage parents to classify their children's behaviors as Class One, Class Two, or Class Three behaviors. If it's a Class One behavior, then it is extremely important. Class One behaviors usually revolve around safety issues. For instance, it is very important to me that my toddler not run out into the street or put his fingers in the light socket. It is very important to me that my teenager does not drink or ride in a car with those who do.

Class Two behaviors reflect important family values—matters of the heart. Consistency in enforcing these boundaries is important, because these behaviors reflect our family's values and priorities. For instance, it is important to my husband and me that our children practice compassion, charity, and respect for others. It's important to us that we attend church as a family. Our children will have housekeeping responsibilities, and they will tithe on their allowances. Boundaries set around Class Two behaviors reflect the importance of those issues to the family.

Class Three behaviors are somewhat important to me, but I may not be as vigilant in enforcing them as I am at enforcing other behaviors. These are the "it would be nice if" kinds of behaviors. They are not safety issues, and they don't necessarily speak to our family priorities. They are just things I'd like my children to do. For example, I would like my kids to keep their bedrooms clean, but there is room for interpretation as to what "clean" means. I would like my children to look neat when they leave the house, but I can allow for some modest personal-statement-making in the way they dress. It's important to pinpoint the Class Three behaviors because these boundaries can be wider than those for Class One and Two behaviors.

Limits that are firm make children feel more comfortable, even safer. Limits that are weak or that fall apart easily make children feel unsafe and insecure. Many behavioral studies have been done to prove this, but you need no further proof than to see a child act out in the face of no boundaries.

> *Limits that are firm make children feel more comfortable, even safer. Limits that are weak make children feel unsafe and insecure.*

I sat next to a woman on an airplane once who had a beautiful four-year-old boy named Spencer and some very weak personal boundaries. Whenever she would say "no" to him, which she did often, little Spencer would throw a tantrum and (you guessed it) would get what he had demanded in the first place. I couldn't help but feel sorry—not for her, so much, but for him. The little guy was blinded by the power his mother had given him to get what he wanted when he wanted it. Because of the countless times in the past that she let him run over her personal and behavioral boundaries, Spencer was a horse without a fence, running wild. He was behaviorally unsure and therefore felt unsafe. What he really wanted was a boundary— an absolute no followed by a loving but firm consequence for disobedience. He may not have liked it, but he would have felt safer and perhaps been able to calm down and enjoy the trip.

Children crave boundaries. If you haven't set a needed boundary, your children will often try to force you to do so by acting out and misbehaving. They misbehave in order to "feel around" for the boundary line, much like groping for the light switch in a darkened room. They need to know where you stand and that, just like God our Father, you stand there consistently.

Some parents go beyond setting strong boundaries. They are so afraid of their children making mistakes that they arrange their children's lives to eliminate the opportunity to disobey. But if children never have a chance to disobey, they are not really learning to obey. Parents who micromanage their children by telling them the exact way to do everything are robbing them of countless opportunities for struggle and growth.

As much as we might want to protect our children from making mistakes and having to bear the consequences, this is not God's style. In the Garden of Eden, God the Father showed His children the tree of the knowledge of good and evil and then told them not to eat its fruit (Genesis 2:17). God never takes away all temptation; rather, He makes sure we see the temptation and that we know where the boundary lines lie. Then He is there as the loving parent to administer the appropriate consequences, whether we stay in the boundaries or leave them.

We also need to make a distinction here between setting a boundary for children's behavior and expecting children to "walk the straight and narrow." Requiring children to live within unreasonably narrow boundaries is setting them up for failure. Childhood is the mistake-making period of their lives. It is unreasonable to expect a child to adhere to a strict code of behavior that insists he do things the way his parents would do them. Boundaries are intended to be freeing, not stifling. A boundary should be broad enough to allow a child to make good choices. The goal is not to draw a fine line, but rather to give children a defined field in which to work and play.

Requiring children to live within unreasonably narrow boundaries is setting them up for failure.

For example, when you give your child a job to do, tell him what the final product should be, give him a modicum of direction, and then back off and let him do it. If he doesn't go about it in exactly the way you would, that's all right. In fact, that's good. He's finding his own way. In the same way, create behavioral boundaries with enough latitude to allow your children to find their own ways of staying within them.

STICK TO YOUR GUNS

Do not set a boundary that you cannot enforce. For example, you wouldn't want to set the rule, "You must go to sleep at eight o'clock every night." How are you going to make your child go to sleep? Going to sleep is not something she can do on command even if she wanted to. You might say, "You need to be in bed with the lights out at eight," because that you can enforce. Unenforceable boundaries will tear at the stability of all the boundaries you set, because when one crumbles, your children will want to test the strength of the others.

If you have established very few boundaries with your children in the past, you will have a bit of an uphill battle. But the outcome will be well worth the effort. When a parent has not been consistent and then suddenly becomes so, her child is likely to rebel against this new plan. His behavior may actually worsen, causing you to assume that the boundary system didn't work. But stick to your guns. He has the right to hate it, but he doesn't have the right to be disrespectful. You have to remain consistent—sometimes for as long as you have been inconsistent—until your children understand that this boundary system isn't going away.

Set boundaries that will encourage appropriate choice making and discourage inappropriate behavior. Be fair to your children; do not exasperate them by changing the rules in the middle of the game. Boundaries that are unclear or ever changing create an atmosphere that is confusing and can feel unsafe for a child. This type of home atmosphere plays havoc with the development of a child's emotions and his ability to manage his feelings. So above all else, remain consistent.

Where to Begin

You may have difficulty knowing where to start if there are many areas that need boundary setting in your home. Try to stand back from your situation a little and look at it with an objective eye. What are the top two or three behavior problems in your family? Maybe your family isn't working well during transition times such as getting ready for school in the morning or going to bed at night. Start there.

Once you've determined that a certain behavior is important enough to your family to set a boundary, the real work begins. You will need to name the boundary, using as few words as possible. For example, instead of saying, "When we get in the car to go somewhere, you must first obey me by putting on your seat belt and getting settled down before you can ask for a toy or a book," simply say "First you obey and then you play." Short and sweet—sound bites. "First you obey and then you play" actually covers many areas of concern. When your children get older, the same idea can be communicated by saying, "You have to pay to play."

You will also need to think through and communicate what you will do if your child doesn't respect the boundary and what you will do if she does. The basic theme when considering consequences is that if your child doesn't control herself, then you need to step in and control her. This needs to be stated clearly and often. "If you choose not to control yourself, then you are asking me to control you." Once this is established verbally, many a child will test it out in the real world. And you will need to be standing right there on the boundary line when she does.

Keep the consequences for leaving the boundary lines as natural as possible. If a child is careless with someone else's property and something is broken, he must either fix it or pay for it. If a child is late for curfew, the curfew gets moved forward an hour or two. If a child is acting out at the table, he gets to eat by himself.

> *Keep the consequences for leaving the boundary lines as natural as possible.*

Be clear with your words. Be clear with your actions. Observe your children to determine what triggers good choices and what triggers poor choices. Set your boundaries accordingly. If, for instance, your children are consistently making poor choices at the dinner table, you need to set a boundary for behavior there. You will notice that your child makes better choices when you give him feedback about how he's doing.

Knowing Where You Stand

Throughout the Scriptures, God worked to make the boundary lines clear to His children. The Father knows that if His children are to learn the boundaries, He must teach us clearly and consistently and constantly. God never seeks to trick His children or to catch us in disobedience. He doesn't watch from afar, ready to clobber us when we mess up. This is not His style. He wants us to make good choices, just as we want our children to make good choices. In order to support His children in their efforts to stay within the bounds of His design, God continually calls us to a standard of living that can be sustained only by our complete reliance on Him. When we are listening to Him, seeking Him, paying attention to Him, He does not hesitate to make His expectations clear, consistent, and constant.

Likewise, we must be sure to continuously talk about the boundary lines we have set in our home, giving feedback as to how each child is doing. Statements such as "You're making great choices; I'm proud of you" or "Way to go! You stayed way inbounds even though you were angry" communicate to a child that he is doing fine. On the other hand, if a child is having trouble staying in the boundaries, feedback such as "You're out-of-bounds. You need to get back inbounds" or "You're right on the boundary line; better come back in" encourages a child to change his behavior or expect consequences. Be sure to first give the child a chance to come back in the boundary lines before you discipline him. The goal here is to encourage wise behavior, not to catch him in unwise behavior.

REAL BOUNDARIES DON'T SHIFT

What happens when your children are getting dangerously close to the boundary line? The answer to this question will say a lot about our ability to make our boundaries firm. Let's say the boundary is that my child needs to respond to my request the first time I ask. I ask her to do something and she responds, "Just a minute." She is standing on the boundary line, seriously considering stretching her big toe into the land of disobedience. If I respond to this by warning her, "You'd better not disobey me!" or by that age-old parental tactic, "I'm going to give you five seconds to obey. One, two, three, four, four and a half, four and three quarters…" then the boundary line shifts from where I had originally said it was. And believe me, she notices!

If we warn them at all, it needs to be one reminder of where the boundary line lies and where they are in relation to it. Parents who continuously warn their children to comply find that their children wait until the last warning is given to follow through. Why is this? Because that is where the boundary line actually lies. Some children are better than others about seeing that invisible line, but when we warn continuously and delay following through with consequences, we teach our children not to respect our boundaries.

In- and Out-of-Bounds

Our children may have heard the word *boundary* in school when talking about the line between two states or countries. A boundary line is set up so that we will know where one place ends and another begins. We have boundary lines in most sports so that we know when a player or the ball is inbounds or out-of-bounds. As we set personal and behavioral boundaries at home, we are in essence doing the same thing. The boundary lines we draw help our children know where the place called *obedience* ends, and when they've entered the territory called *disobedience*.

The boundary lines we draw help our children know where the place called obedience ends, and when they've entered the territory called disobedience.

Anna was a second grader who was having recess trouble. By mid-year no one wanted to play with her much anymore. The teachers were concerned but also confused, since Anna was a well-liked child in the classroom. She was great at sports, imaginative, energetic—what's not to like? Upon closer examination, the teachers realized why she was having so much trouble. Anna was creating wonderfully imaginative games to play at recess, complete with rules and regulations. The games were fun, and many of the children had entered into play willingly. The problem was that Anna would change the rules of the game midstream. Every so often the boundary lines would shift and only she would know where they were. It didn't take long for the children to realize that they not only couldn't win at this game, but they couldn't even enjoy playing it. They cried "Not fair!"—and indeed, it wasn't fair.

The same is true as we parent. It seems arbitrary to a child when it is only after they are out-of-bounds that we tell them where the boundary line is. It is unfair to set boundaries retroactively. If you haven't drawn the boundary of "no PG-13 movies" for your preteen, it is unreasonable for you to punish him for viewing one. However, this might be a good time to set the boundary for the next time he has a choice of what movie to watch.

It is important to children that they know where they stand. This is the beauty of using phrases such as "You're inbounds" or "You're out-of-bounds" when talking about their behavior. Life progresses much more smoothly when everyone knows what is expected of them. Boundaries need to be consistent and predictable. If boundaries keep changing, it's frustrating to everyone. It would be like trying to play a game where the rules keep changing.

- Can you think of a personal boundary you may need to establish? Are there some personal boundaries you have set for yourself that involve your children in some way? How do you plan to communicate those personal boundaries to them?

- What are some behavioral boundaries that you have set but not enforced? What has been the consequence of this? What do you need to do in order to reestablish that boundary?

- Name three or four Class One behaviors in your family. Name three or four Class Two behaviors. Name three or four Class Three behaviors.

- How can you encourage your children to set personal boundaries for themselves? What might you do that would discourage them from doing this?

Chapter Four

LIFE IN ABUNDANCE

When my daughter Anna Kate was a toddler she went on several "playdates" with another two-year-old named Rachel. A playdate is a previously arranged time when two young children get together and completely ignore each other as they play next to, but not with, each other. This was supposed to build social skills, I think. The girls, however, were not socially compatible. Anna Kate's philosophy in life was—and continues to be— "What's mine is yours and what's yours is mine." (When she gets older this will be labeled a lack of personal boundaries, but it worked for her when she was two.) Rachel's mantra was more like "What's mine is mine and leave me and mine alone!" When it was Rachel's turn to host the playdate, life got a bit complicated. Because they were *her* toys, Rachel spent the entire time clutching tightly to any and every toy she could hold and repeating "Mine!" with varying levels of intensity. No matter how much her mother encouraged her to share her toys, Rachel could not relax her grip on what was hers long enough to enjoy the playdate. Of course, Rachel grew out of that stage, but at the time, her fear of losing her possessions stifled her ability to enjoy them.

We adults sometimes get a "Mine!" mentality about our possessions and our time. Both are precious commodities to us. We sometimes think of God's provision of possessions and time as just enough to get by, but the abundance of life God offers us is actually likened to a feast in the Bible (Luke 14:15–24). His gifts to His children are lavish, and He invites us to feast on the beauty and intensity of life. But there is a distinct difference between feasting and just plain being a glutton. When we feast, we partake, we fellowship, we enjoy. When we act in gluttony, we hoard, we compete, we take. We must teach our children to appreciate what they have—to manage their money and their belongings—and to recognize and reject their gluttonous desires for more and more, accepting instead their Father's standing invitation to the real feast.

> *We must teach our children to appreciate what they have and to recognize and reject their gluttonous desires for more and more.*

THE DANGER OF TOO MUCH

Mark's teacher was the first to notice it. He was having great difficulty getting along with his peers. He didn't want to play the games they wanted to play. At recess, he wanted everyone to play only the games he devised. When things didn't go his way, he wanted a "do-over." He even tried to buy some friends by bringing toys from home and giving them to those who promised to be his friend. It was clear that Mark had no idea how to make, keep, or be a friend.

When the school called his parents to come in for a conference, his mom and dad were not surprised. Apparently, Mark had difficulty with the neighborhood children as well. His parents reported that he seemed unhappy and insecure. They just couldn't understand Mark's difficulties because they had done everything they knew to give him all he needed or wanted. He had an abundance of natural intelligence, of attention from his parents, of toys and games and entertainment. But, as much as they wanted him to be out playing with friends, he always ended up playing video games or in his room by himself. Because his toys and games were far superior and more plentiful than those of his friends, he rarely wanted to go to anyone else's home to play. When friends did come over, they usually ended up playing separately with Mark's abundance of toys and possessions.

The good news was that Mark wanted friends. He was aware enough to know he was missing out on the relationships others enjoyed. The bad news was that the abundance of his possessions was actually keeping him from what he desired most—friendship.

How much is too much? Is it wrong to give our children the things they want—to offer them an abundance of entertainment, freedom, and fun? Our children don't have to ask us to feed them, clothe them, or educate them. We provide these things for them without their asking. The things they usually ask for are the things that there can, indeed, be too much of: Can I watch TV? Can I be on the computer? Can I have this magazine? Can we play video games? Can we go to the mall?

The generation of children now entering young adulthood has grown up with the disadvantages of abundance that people my age didn't have. We didn't have to juggle the overabundance of possessions that children juggle today. We didn't have the constant pull of the Internet enticing us to look, to listen, and to experience. We didn't have the option of escaping into a video game when life got tough. Our choices were fewer, our enticements were limited, and for this I am grateful.

We have to find a way to teach our children the dangers of these pursuits while at the same time teaching them to make good and reasonable choices regarding how they spend time in them. My children find it hard to know when they have had enough fun, enough of a sport, enough junk food, or enough time being entertained. It is nearly impossible for my children to know when they have played *enough* video games or watched *enough* TV. I could keep them away from such fun altogether, but this wouldn't teach them the important lesson of knowing when to stop. Part of living in a world of abundance is knowing when you have had enough. I would like my children to learn the advice of the quintessential child specialist, Mary Poppins, when she said, "Enough is as good as a feast." So true. In fact, enough is better than a feast, because all of the excess— all of the abundance—becomes a burden to me once I have genuinely had enough.

Part of living in a world of abundance is knowing when you have had enough.

Sometimes an abundance of entertainment is simply unnecessary; at other times, it's downright harmful. When children spend too much time with electronics—video games, computer, television, DVDs, and videos—they have less practice at developing language skills and relationships with other children or with family. While playing organized sports can have a wonderful influence on a child, sports offer few opportunities to problem-solve creatively or to resolve conflict, because there are always rules and referees and adults around to mediate any differences. As a result, today's children have unprecedented difficulty in knowing how to communicate their ideas, their thoughts, and their feelings. Even more disturbing are the problems many children have relating to one another, solving conflict, and cooperating with each other. When children of any age spend much of their time in parallel play—that is, playing independently but *next* to each other and not *with* each other— they simply don't have the experiences they need in learning how to be in relationship.

God our Father teaches us time and again in the Scriptures that life is about relationship—with Him and with each other. He draws a clear boundary line between living for our possessions and using them to benefit others as we live for Him. When we store up treasures on earth, we run the great risk of missing the point in life (Matthew 6:19). Likewise, when our children's treasures draw them into play that does not encourage relationship, they, too, run the risk of missing the point in life.

GETTING IN THE WAY OF THE REAL GIFTS

God is clear on the subject of wealth. He intends for us to provide for our families and to be fiscally responsible both in the present and in saving for future needs. But just as importantly, we are to spread our abundance around, to use what we have to bless others, to be more concerned about relationships than about having lots of stuff. You see, God made us for relationships, not for stuff. If God has given your family more than you need, then it might be because there's another family with less than they need with whom God may want you to share, and in doing so, establish a relationship. In 1 Timothy 6, we get a clear picture of what it means to be "rich in good deeds." Here our Father paints a clear picture of how much more fulfilling it is to be rich in relationships than it is to simply be rich in possessions. Take some time to talk as a family about the ways you can use your abundance of things to build relationships with and to help others.

Our family has several friends who use the abundance of their possessions to bless others. Although we will never know the level of wealth they enjoy, we are encouraged by their repeated displays of generosity. What a priceless example to my children, not only to witness people being generous, but also to learn how to be a gracious recipient of that generosity. We want our children to bless others with what they have, but we also want them to know how to graciously receive blessing from others, knowing that the originator of all wealth is God their Father. Sometimes He chooses to bless us not by giving us wealth but by allowing others the opportunity to be generous to us with the wealth He has given them.

We want our children to bless others with what they have, but we also want them to know how to graciously receive blessing from others.

Just like our children, we have many chances to choose things over people, and we often do. But when we choose to go out of the boundaries of how we are to use the earthly treasures God has given, we forfeit something. The Father lovingly warns His children that those who cling to worthless idols forfeit the grace that could be theirs (Jonah 2:8). When we hold tightly to possessions, to the things money can buy, we give away some of the time and the connectedness with others—the grace of life—that money can't buy. I certainly don't want to forfeit any grace God has for me or for my children in exchange for the things that will not last, but every day I must make a conscious choice about this. I need to recognize when I have had enough so I can teach my children to recognize when they have had enough.

The More We Have, the More We Want

We live in a strange world. We live in a world where people have an abundance of food and carry on a constant battle with their weight, while others just a few blocks away are starving. We live in a world where children long to go to school but must work, and where other children must be bribed and cajoled into going to school. We live in a world where some people cannot make enough money to support their families no matter how many jobs they hold, and other people, living nearby, can retire at thirty because they have all the money they will ever need. What a weird world.

I don't know about you, but our family lives somewhere in between. Because of the off-balance society we live in, we think of *abundance* as referring to excessive consumerism and ostentatious greed. A truer definition of *abundance* is simply that there is more than enough. Given this definition, everybody I know lives in abundance, and I'll bet you do as well.

Jesus tells us, "Watch out! Be on your guard against all kinds of greed; a man's life does not consist in the abundance of his possessions" (Luke 12:15). We who have an abundance of things need to be on our guard against greed, against covetousness. It seems that the more we have, the more we want. If we get the new DVD player, it won't be long before we'll want the plasma TV and the surround-sound system that was advertised with it. A new sofa in the living room just makes it all the more obvious that the curtains need replacing, too. It never ends.

And even though Jesus' words remind us that our lives are not defined by the abundance of our possessions, we still tend to define ourselves that way. We are a middle-income family. We live in this or that neighborhood. We drive this or that kind of car. Too often we slip into the thinking that the more our family has, the more esteemed we will be, the more secure we will be, and the more influential we will be. These are nothing but illusions that we, even as Christians, have adopted as truth and that often guide the lives of our families. God knows that when we base our vision of ourselves on how much money we make, we leave ourselves vulnerable to every manner of dissatisfaction, resentment, and greed. He doesn't want us to sell ourselves short looking for wealth we can see, all the while overlooking the plentiful quantities of hope and joy and life in abundance that only He can give. We may say we don't believe that possessions define our lives, but wouldn't we, like the rich young ruler, hang our heads and walk away if Jesus asked us to sell everything we had and give it to the poor (Matthew 19:16–24)?

THE GIVER OF ALL GOOD GIFTS

Like many of you, my husband and I worry that the abundance in which we live—where there is plenty (and then some) of everything—may be damaging to our children. We want our children to recognize God as the Provider of everything we need and as the generous Giver of all that we enjoy in this life. This truth is central to the gospel and to our reliance on Him as Father.

We want our children to recognize God as the Provider of everything we need and as the generous Giver of all that we enjoy in this life.

As God's child, I am sure that He will provide for my needs. He has promised you and me that He will never fail in this parental responsibility (Matthew 6:33). In fact, He often gives us more than we need (James 1:17). In the same way, we provide for our own children, and we often enjoy giving them more than they need. I love that feeling of giving my children a wonderful gift that they aren't expecting, don't you? God does, too. Our Father enjoys giving His children good gifts far more than we will ever know (Matthew 7:9–11).

So how do we know when the gifts we give our children are good and right and when they become ostentatious and over the top? The answer is not in the gift itself, but rather in the way our children react to and use the gift. God never says that enjoying abundance or wealth is wrong. He says instead that the love of money and a devotion to wealth are wrong. Not only wrong, but *a root of all kinds of evil* (1 Timothy 6:10). We children need to pay attention to God's strong words here. Why is God so adamant that we not become enticed and preoccupied by the accumulation of earthly treasures? For the same reason we are adamant that our children not become enticed and preoccupied by their earthly treasures—because they take us away from each other. If the abundance of our possessions is not being used to provide for our family, to provide for the needs of others, or to further God's kingdom in some way, then we have misused God's gifts to us.

Even more important, when we are paying attention to our things, we are not paying attention to God. Living with an abundance of things can blur our vision of God and of what we are on this earth to do. When we spend all our time and energy earning, accumulating, and maintaining our possessions, we are not spending that time with others, and we may be ignoring the mission God has called us to. What's more, it is by watching us that our children develop the value systems they will live under even as adults. I don't know what God's plan is for your life, but I'm sure it's not for you to store up earthly treasures. As we teach our children that people are more important than things, we teach them that in God's economy, relationships—with Him and with others—are the treasures. And God's treasures don't break. They don't rust or deteriorate or get stolen or have to be insured. An abundance of these treasures is worth storing up (Matthew 6:19–20).

LIFE IN ABUNDANCE

When Jesus said that He came to give life and to give it abundantly (John 10:10), what did He mean, exactly? My mother-in-law once explained to me that the abundance Jesus promises consists of the good, the bad, and the ugly of life—all in abundance. Jesus didn't come to give us an abundance of only the happy and pleasant life, because that would not be life to the full. Love and arguments and relationships and good times and hard times and fun and work and laughter and tears—these are what make up real life.

God's gift of abundant life comes in the level of participation that we experience when we live in faith. Our emotions, our senses, our understandings are all heightened to a level far beyond what we could ever hope for without faith in our Father. Deeply in love with His children, God gives *more than enough* grace, mercy, compassion, healing, care, wisdom, patience, and, most important, love.

> *Deeply in love with His children,*
> *God gives more than enough grace, mercy,*
> *compassion, healing, care, wisdom, patience,*
> *and, most important, love.*

As parents, we recognize that parenting itself is a round-the-clock, nonstop, intense experience in the high highs and the low lows of life. Raising children is heavily loaded with emotion—joy, pain, uncertainty—all in abundance. We have deeper feelings for our children than we do about most anything else in life. We invest more time and energy and money in our family relationships than we ever thought possible. The roller-coaster experience of parenting enables us to participate in a whole new level of life—abundant life. This is the abundance Jesus spoke of; any financial resources we may have pale in comparison.

Ask your children what they have in abundance. They will probably answer food, clothes, money, and toys, and they will be right. But the stuff that makes life real and abundant has nothing to do with stuff. Our children need to understand that the things they have can be tools used in loving and helping each other. Their toys are more than just toys; they are tools they can use to love their friends and siblings. Your home is more than just a home; it is a peaceful refuge for your family and provides a way to bless others with your hospitality and graciousness.

Our children must see us refusing to put our hope in our wealth but rather putting our hope in God—and enjoying His rich provision of treasures, which wealth could never buy.

Assessing Intangible Wealth

The Petersons have an abundance of children. Their Christmas cards are awe-inspiring as they display the beauty of such a large and yet cohesive family. They don't have an abundance of earthly possessions, yet they live out of the abundance of the love and genuine care they have for others. While their children certainly enjoy being involved in sports and fine arts opportunities, they understand that the relationships within the family and those friendships God has blessed them with are a priority. The Petersons do not see themselves as lacking just because they cannot compete in the world's economy; they are wealthy in God's economy, where possessions such as graciousness, peace, unselfishness, and integrity are more prized than anything.

Have you ever fantasized about being wealthier than you

are right now? My husband and I have. Sometimes it's fun; sometimes it's depressing. Nevertheless, when we imagine not having to worry about budgeting or taxes or paying for the roof to be replaced, we envision having more time with our family. We imagine that we would take the Sabbath more seriously— basking luxuriously in the restfulness of no worries—and that we would give more to the needs of others. When we return to reality—to our current financial status—we realize there is really nothing stopping us from living in that kind of abundance right now. We can spend more time with our family right now. We can take more Sabbath rests to restore ourselves, resting in the security of God's assurances. We can give much to the needs of others. Our gifts may not all be material, but as a family, we still have much to give.

Most of us assess our financial status regularly. We create budgets, financial plans, and portfolios. We keep a record of the possessions in our homes for insurance purposes, and every year at tax time we know exactly how much money we made last year, even if we don't know where it all went. We give much attention to the abundance of our tangible possessions, but we seldom assess our more important, intangible possessions.

What are the things your family has in abundance that are not tangible? You may have an abundance of love for others and for each other. You may have an abundance of patience or kindness or compassion for those in need. You might have an abundance of knowledge or expertise in an area that would be beneficial to someone else. You may have an abundance of time available to spend with those who have no one. As a family you have more than enough God-given gifts you can use to bless and help others.

As a family you have more than
enough God-given gifts you can use
to bless and help others.

So how do we keep an assessment of our intangible wealth? Much like we do our tangible wealth—by paying attention to it. Along with our children, we can begin a list of what we have in abundance. Does our family have plenty of mercy and concern for those in need? Do we have time to spare that could be shared with others? Do we enjoy lots of laughter and enjoyment that encourages those around us? Maybe we have special skills we could use to benefit others. Perhaps we'll keep the list on the refrigerator and add to it as things come to mind. And while doing so, we can remind each other to look to our Father not only for the gifts themselves but also for the eyes to see these gifts in the fullness of their importance to Him.

As God's children we are free to enjoy His abundant gifts and to rejoice in His provision, whether He gives to us or to someone else. We recognize that when God gives to His children, His intention is never for us to hoard and covet those gifts but to use them in ways that provide for needs and build relationships. We parents are continuously learning this lesson as we seek to teach it in turn to our children. In doing so, we also teach them to appraise not just the tangible gifts God gives but also those intangible, often more important gifts. Perhaps one of our most cherished gifts is the experience of life that comes when we parent our children in full awareness of being parented by God our Father.

CONSIDER THIS...

- What earthly possessions or wealth has God given you? In what ways do you think He would have you use your wealth to bless others? In what ways does your earthly wealth get in the way of helping others?

- What tangible or intangible gifts that you do not currently have would you like to have in abundance in your family? How would this help your family? How might you work toward this goal?

- What is your evaluation of your intangible possessions? Have you discovered gifts your family didn't realize it had? How has the recognition of these treasures changed the perspective your family has of itself?

Chapter Five

THE LESSONS
OF CHOICE

For the first time in his life, our five-year-old got a check from a relative for his birthday. Having only recently begun to appreciate the power of money, he didn't quite know what to think. We assured him that he would get to turn that money into a gift of his choice at the nearby toy store. He was so excited he could hardly contain himself. In the days leading up to our big toy-store venture, he spent many moments daydreaming about what he might buy.

With his check cashed and ten dollars in hand, we blissfully headed out for the toy store. What a day this would be! Not only would he get to choose his birthday present, but we would get the added pleasure of teaching him how to make the most of his money. It was a win-win.

As with most parental expectations, this one was soon dashed. As soon as we entered the toy store, we could see that look come over our son's face—that "this is way too much for my young brain to handle" look. We guided him to an aisle with the under-ten-dollar toys and began to suggest aloud some possible choices for him. It seemed as though he was taking it in fairly well when suddenly his face began to redden, tears welled up in his eyes, and with a quavering voice he asked, "Will you choose for me?"

In hindsight, we should have known better. Children often have difficulty when faced with too many choices. Recognizing this, we chose five toys within his price range, and after recovering some composure, he was able to choose from there. We celebrated his choice with him—even though in our opinion it was not the best buy for his money—and we made a mental note to never do that again to a five-year-old.

> *Children often have difficulty when*
> *faced with too many choices.*

Paper or plastic? Video or DVD? Latte or mocha? MCI or Sprint? Living in this free-market society in which competition between businesses is fierce, we're offered choice upon choice upon choice. Even our youngest children are targeted by these advertisements. Not only do advertisers want us to make a choice—their product—but they also want to convince us that we deserve to have a choice. For many years, our society has been communicating—no, shouting—the message that we have an inalienable right to choose for ourselves anything and everything, from the brand of peanut butter we like to the brand of theology we prefer. This enticing message can be a particular problem for children. They already have a mind-boggling number of choices to make every day. Many are inconsequential and even trivial; others are life altering and permanent.

The fundamental problem is not that we have too many choices but rather that we have the power of choice at all. I suppose we cannot call this a problem, because it is God's design. He is the One who entrusted His children with this liberating and binding, beautiful and dangerous gift of choice.

Sometimes I look around at the effects of the millions of poor choices made in the world every day, including my own, and I wonder to myself, *What was God thinking?* Didn't He know what a mess His children would make of free will? Didn't He know that we don't have the maturity or the character required to make even the simplest of good choices? Of course He did know, and He does know.

At the most basic level, God our Parent has given us—and our children—the gift of free will so that we have the option of choosing to love and serve Him. This is His great hope; this is our only hope. But free will is not limited to this one all-important decision. The freedom to choose permeates every thought we think, every word we say. God allows us this freedom and gives us ample opportunity to practice it—opportunities to make good choices and poor choices. As we take a look at some of the ways He teaches us about, and through, our freedom of choice, we recognize some of the avenues through which we can teach our own children about choice.

TEACHING CHOICE-MAKING

God recognizes that His children have great difficulty making good choices, but He also recognizes that He can use our poor choices as a means of teaching and training us. Time and time again, as God parented the Israelites of the Old Testament, He had to deal with their poor choices. The cycle repeats itself again and again—God blessed His people; they became complacent and selfish and rebellious; God withheld His blessings and allowed neighboring nations to rule over them; they called out to God for forgiveness and deliverance; God forgave, delivered, and blessed them; they became complacent and selfish…and on and on the cycle goes. I don't know about you, but this is a pattern in my life as well. What is our Father to do with us?

As we guide our children through their countless poor choices, we must remember that God has provided for them in the same way He has provided for us. He redeems and uses their poor choices in much the same way that He does our own. He does not shield us from the consequences of our choices, nor should we shield our children from the consequences of theirs. God even makes creative use of the choices both we and our children have made in disobedience. In parenting the Israelites, God the Father continued to give them choices even in light of their childishness and disobedience. He did not resort—as we often do—to micromanaging His children. He parented and disciplined them, but He did not control them. In His wisdom, He knows that no growth or maturity results from being overly controlled. He may limit the choices He gives, but He still allows His children to choose.

God does not shield us from the consequences of our choices, nor should we shield our children from the consequences of theirs.

It may be difficult for us to know when it is and isn't appropriate to allow a child to choose. For example, it is appropriate to allow a five-year-old to choose between three outfits to wear, but it is inappropriate to allow her to order what she wants for dinner every night. Good nutrition is not a concept that a five-year-old can understand.

If we allow a child to make choices he is not developmentally ready to make, there are several possible results. First, he is likely to make very unwise choices. When a child is allowed to choose his own bedtime, for instance, he will probably stay up too late and so be cranky and listless the next day. Second, he may get anxious and fretful over being faced with a choice. If you see signs of fear or nervousness, your child may need you to help him understand the choices or maybe even limit those choices for him. Finally, he may choose unrealistically. A child might want to play football, basketball, and soccer all at the same time, not understanding the time constraints involved.

God our Parent knows when to let us make our own decisions and when to intervene. How does He know? He knows because He so thoroughly knows us. Likewise, we must stay keenly aware of our children's development, their personalities, and their perspectives so we can discern when to back away and when to intervene in their choice making.

LIMITING THEIR CHOICES

God's model for developing our ability to make choices involves continually giving us choices and at the same time limiting those choices. God gave Adam and Eve the choice of the fruit of any tree in the Garden of Eden, but He limited their choice by telling them there was one tree they could not eat from (Genesis 2:16–17). They made a poor choice anyway. Jesus gave each disciple the invitation to deny himself, take up his cross, and follow Him (Matthew 16:24). Most of them made a good choice. Occasionally God allows us a startling degree of freedom. Perhaps He does this when He knows we are ready to make an independent choice, or at other times because He wants to teach us to seek His input when making a decision. Either way, He teaches us to make good choices by first asking us to be faithful in the smaller choices—the limited choices—and then giving us larger and weightier decisions to make as we grow in maturity and faith (Matthew 25:21).

In situations where a choice is the child's to make, parents can help him make a wise choice by limiting his options. Our son's toy-store nightmare was salvaged only because we limited his options so that he was able to choose for himself. Even though it was a mistake for us to give him so many choices to begin with, it would also have been a mistake to tell him what to buy. Giving no choice and giving too many choices have similar effects, and neither teaches a child to make wise choices.

> *Giving no choice and giving too many choices have similar effects, and neither teaches a child to make wise choices.*

Of course, what happens *after* a choice is made is also important. We may point out alternatives for him to consider, but in the end we should be willing to accept his decision, if it is anywhere within the limits of reason. When we question our child's choice too strongly, he learns to doubt his decision-making ability and will have a harder time making choices in the future.

I am seeing a disturbing trend in many families today. Some children have great difficulty making decisions because their parents, rather than teaching them how to make good choices, have taught them *not* to make choices at all. Why would a parent do this? When parents are so concerned that every choice be right, that no opportunity be missed, they often fall into the trap of making all the decisions for the child. The child is simply a bystander in the decision-making process, missing a golden opportunity to learn a crucial skill.

Although some decisions must be made solely by the parents, many decisions can and must involve the children if they are to develop experience in making choices. Perhaps we will let our daughter choose to wear the pink striped shirt with the red polka-dot shorts. Maybe we should let our son go out for the basketball team even though he is the shortest boy in his class. When assigning a task to accomplish, we might tell him what we want the end result to be but not how to go about accomplishing it; we will let him choose his own method.

On the other hand, with important family decisions, such as what school a child will attend or whether the family will move to a different city, a child should never be put into the position of being the major decision-maker. This causes unfair stress on the child, since children are developmentally unable to make life-changing decisions with wisdom. We need to say to the child, "This is not your decision. Mom and Dad are going to make the final choice, but we would like to know what you think about it." This puts the child at ease and offers great opportunity to hear her thoughts and feelings.

Also, children need to learn to trust their parents' decisions for them. If we give them a choice at every turn, they begin to believe that it is not their parents' role to make choices on their behalf. In fact, it is often the parents' responsibility to make choices for their children, and it must be exercised regularly. Our goal is to build the children's confidence so they can make good decisions—or at least acceptable decisions—and to teach them the important lesson that not all choices are of equal importance. God does not desire for us to be mindless servants, just waiting for the next command from the Master; nor do we want our children to sleepwalk through life, allowing us to make all the decisions for them. We want them to think independently and to learn to make good choices.

> *Our goal is to build the children's confidence so they can make good decisions.*

Lucy

Lucy likes to do everything right—the first time. She does not like to try out new activities because she may not be good at them. Consequently, she passes up opportunities to participate with her friends in different sports and social and church activities. Her social skills are beginning to be affected, because as her friends grow and change, they want to pursue new interests while Lucy does not. She is becoming increasingly bored with life but still resists venturing out. More and more of Lucy's idle hours are spent at home playing by herself. Her parents do not think she is making good choices but don't know whether it is healthy to push her to try new things. So they move back and forth between forcing her to participate in new activities, and allowing her to "be herself" with pastimes she's sure she can do well.

If Lucy continues to avoid healthy risks, she is likely to develop difficulties in school as well. She will be reluctant to participate in class because she won't want to risk giving the wrong answer. As she gets older, she may even choose easier classes and a less challenging career as a way of ensuring that she will be successful. Lucy is setting a pattern of poor choice making at an early age.

In working with Lucy's parents, I reminded them that God first considers the motives of the heart (1 Samuel 16:7). I challenged them to consider their motives in wanting Lucy to participate more in different activities. Was it because they thought they had a budding sports star? Was it because it just "looked weird" for a child to prefer playing at home by herself? We earthly parents can be tempted to push our children in directions that seem right, but for all the wrong reasons. However, it was clear that Lucy was setting some unhealthy patterns for herself and needed the intervention of her parents.

As we discussed her schedule, taking into account homework, family responsibilities, and the need for time alone, it was clear that she still had ample time to participate in a few after-school activities. We decided that Lucy's parents would talk with her about healthy risk-taking and how important it is to try new activities, even if she did not feel competent, explaining that participation is often more important than success. They made a deal with Lucy that she would participate in one activity in which she felt confident and in one activity in which she was unsure of herself. Her parents allowed Lucy to choose these activities, but they made sure that one of each type was chosen.

Now, after several months, Lucy has begun to take other healthy risks, knowing that choosing to participate did not bring with it an expectation of success or stardom. Lucy feels more comfortable in the classroom as well, participating in class discussions and group projects without the self-imposed expectation of perfection. Lucy has begun to learn how to make good choices regarding how she spends her time.

SOWING AND REAPING

Throughout the Scriptures, God the Parent teaches the laws of sowing and reaping—of choice making and consequences (Job 4:8; 2 Corinthians 9:6). It is so difficult for us parents to let our children reap the consequences of their poor choices. But we rob them of a clear understanding of this crucial truth when we let them sow irresponsibility and reap freedom, when we let them sow disrespect and reap leniency. If a child sows disobedience, he should not expect to reap joy by getting what he wants.

> *It is so difficult for us parents*
> *to let our children reap the consequences*
> *of their poor choices.*

The most effective consequences are those that arise naturally from the situation. Some poor choices have built-in and immediate consequences—touch a hot stove and you will feel pain, hit another child and he will probably hit you back, play carelessly with your toys and they will break. Other poor choices call for parents to devise a consequence that is as closely related to the offense as possible.

For example, if a child intentionally breaks her brother's toy, the consequence is that she must pay to replace it. Even if the child is very young, she must do small chores around the house to "earn" the money from her parents to replace the toy. If a child intentionally offends someone, he must apologize. Letters or pictures of apology work well because while the child works on the project, he has time to consider his poor choice. For older children, acting in an untrustworthy manner brings the consequence of losing independence—not going out with friends, not driving the car.

Many parents get into the rut of assigning the same punishment for every poor choice a child makes. Spanking, especially, can easily become the one-size-fits-all punishment in some families. Yelling, fussing, nagging, and shaming are common practices that are rarely effective and are always damaging to the child and to the parent-child relationship.

We need to distinguish between poor choices made from childish indiscretion and those made from outright defiance. When a child makes a defiant choice, he must be punished. But most of the poor choices a child makes are rooted in childish indiscretion and require a different approach.

When a child's poor choice warrants a consequence, it is important that we have a plan for administering consequences that are simple, consistent, and as natural as possible. We can adopt a system of natural consequences by first identifying the top three patterns of poor choices we see in our children, then deciding on the consequences ahead of time. For example, if a child consistently "borrows" items from her sister's room without asking, the natural consequence is that she is required to return the item and pay a "rental fee" to her sister. If a teenager abuses the freedom of using the family car, he forfeits the privilege. If he stays out past curfew, he buys himself an evening in his room without electronic entertainment the next time he wants to go somewhere with friends. Most every child goes through a stage in which he consistently makes the unwise choice to delay and complain about doing daily chores. In our home, if you whine and procrastinate about work, you buy yourself more work—and there's always plenty of work to do! Simple. Consistent. Natural.

Finally, we should recognize that our children sometimes make choices that may be poor but are not necessarily moral issues. For example, my daughter may choose to spend her hard-earned money on something I consider to be trivial. My son may choose not to play with a child I believe to be a great kid but whom he simply does not enjoy. We have to be willing to let our children make these kinds of choices.

Our children sometimes make choices that may be poor but are not necessarily moral issues.

Focusing on "consequences" instead of "punishment" helps us to remember that every time our child makes a poor choice, we have an opportunity to train and guide him in God's laws of sowing and reaping. The idea is not simply to stop a specific behavior on a short-term basis, but to train the child to choose well in the future.

STUDYING OUR CHILDREN

God knows us better than we know ourselves. Because He watches over us and knows His children so intimately, He also knows what prompts us to make good choices and poor choices. We can look to Him for wisdom about these patterns in our own lives, asking Him to make us aware of them so that we make more good choices and fewer poor ones.

As we study our children, we will likely see patterns in their choice making. One child may make much better choices when she has time to think them through rather than when she has to make a quick decision. Another child may make poor choices when he is with certain friends. Many children struggle with impulsivity and need adults to help them slow down and consider the situation more fully. Observing our children and learning their patterns enables us to help them learn to watch themselves.

But remember, watching our children make decisions does not mean "helping" them. Making precisely the right decision is not the point; making a good decision *independently* is the point. As we talk to them about what triggers good and poor choices, it is important to maintain a nonjudgmental manner, perhaps by also acknowledging some of our own good and poor choice-making patterns. For instance, you might say, "I have a hard time making a good choice when I haven't stopped to think it through, and I've noticed you have trouble with that, too." When we approach our children with humility and love, they are often more teachable.

THE REWARDS OF GOOD CHOICE

Most of us like to know when we are doing well. We can tell where we stand and so gauge our future choices. Our children also need this feedback. The Bible tells us that God rewards those who diligently seek Him (Hebrews 11:6). When we make the choice to diligently seek God our Parent, He affirms and encourages us. We know we have made some wise parenting choices when we see our children growing and maturing.

Likewise, our children need to know when they have made a right choice. If we notice and comment on the good choice, they are more likely to make that good choice again—"I love the way you said 'thank you' to Grandma," or "You really showed yourself to be a good friend when you let Amy choose the game." Vague or unwarranted praise is not effective with children; we never receive it from Our Father. In keeping with God's example, we bless and teach our children when we notice and acknowledge their good choices and not just their poor choices.

God doesn't use His laws of sowing and reaping just for our poor choices; He uses this system to reward our good choices as well. Peace, for instance, is a natural, built-in result of having regular time alone with God. Progress in a career is a natural result of being diligent in your work and faithful in the stewardship of your gifts. When we sow attentiveness in caring for our garden, we reap a harvest of beautiful flowers, fruits, and vegetables. Simple. Consistent. Natural.

God doesn't use His laws of sowing and reaping just for our poor choices; He uses this system to reward our good choices as well.

Some good choices have built-in positive consequences. Our job as parents is not to contrive rewards, but to help our children to see the naturally occurring results of their wise choices. If your child studies carefully for a test and makes a good grade, the grade—as well as the joy and deserved attention that come with it—is his reward. You may need to point out the connection between the two for him. If your daughter acts responsibly in her use of the family car, then the car will be available to her in the future.

Sometimes a parent needs to design a system of artificial rewards for a child's good choices. These systems might involve a child earning stickers or tokens that add up toward a reward such as extra time playing on the computer or a trip for ice cream. This is necessary only when a parent is trying to develop a certain skill—usually behavioral—for which consequences are too vague or too negative. For example, suppose a child with substantial organizational difficulties is working on gathering all of his materials for homework each afternoon and using his homework planner appropriately. A parent may need to set up an artificial reward system until those skills are built up enough that being organized becomes its own reward. In most cases, however, we can rely on the rewards that result naturally from good choices.

As we watch our children and seek to model God our Parent to them, we must keep in mind one crucial and easily forgotten truth—*they are children*. They are not done yet. They are going to make poor choices each day; that is part of being a child. It is tempting for us to become aggravated and exasperated with them, especially when they make the same poor choices over and over again. Yet, just as God our Parent is willing to give us wisdom generously and without finding fault (James 1:5) when we make the same mistakes over and over, we must patiently give our children wisdom about their choice making—generously and without finding fault. Throughout our children's lives we look for opportunities to pass on the legacy of God's design for life, His wisdom and His character. Perhaps there are no better opportunities to do this than when they make choices.

Consider This...

- What triggers good choice-making in your children? What triggers poor choices? If you have several children, think specifically about each one.

- Is there a way to help them see those patterns of good and poor choice-making without accusing and blaming? How?

- Think of a recent poor choice your child made. What was your reaction to that choice? Did you talk with your child about it? Were there overtones of exasperation or sarcasm in your words? Were you angry? Were you protective or excusing? What lesson about sowing and reaping did your child learn from that experience?

- When your child makes a poor choice, how do you determine the consequences for that choice? What are some ways you can introduce the concept of sowing and reaping by relying on natural consequences in your parenting? Be specific.

Chapter Six

SURPRISED BY ANGER

Recently, our high school girls' basketball team made it to the state semifinal game, which was to be played in a nearby city. The whole school dismissed at 10:30 so that we could all go and cheer on the Lady Lions. My first thought was to send my daughter to the game with a friend so that I could catch up on my never-ending list of things to do. But on second thought, I decided that this could be the memory-making, mother-and-daughter experience I had been recently longing for. After all, Anna Kate had just finished a fun season with her little second-grade basketball team; perhaps it would inspire her to see older girls who love the game so much.

I excitedly told Anna Kate of our plans to leave school early and get lunch on the way to the ballgame, and she seemed pleased. We had a nice drive to the game, although she was much more interested in listening to the radio than in talking to me. At the game we sat with a friend of hers and cheered as our team played valiantly. Everything seemed to be going well.

As we left the arena, however, I noticed a shift in her demeanor. She was sullen and didn't want to hold my hand as we walked. I wondered if she was sad that we lost the game, but she said no. I tried making pleasant conversation, but she countered everything I said with moodiness. I felt my blood pressure rising. As she walked next to me with her arms folded, I mentally totaled up the money and time I had spent on the day. Finally, I stopped her and asked her what was wrong. "I just *want* to act this way," was all she said.

Now, I am no stranger to my daughter's moodiness, but the combination of my having sacrificed much for the day and her having no good reason for being moody sent me right over the edge. As we walked through the parking lot I seriously considered punching a car.

Just what is anger? I know it when I feel it, but it's hard to put into words. The MSN Encarta Encyclopedia defines it as "a feeling of extreme annoyance, a feeling of strong displeasure in response to an assumed injury." That's it! That's why I was so angry with my daughter that day. I was annoyed at her because she had not responded to my efforts as I had wanted or expected, and my feelings were hurt.

When Anger Surprises Us

Raw anger is one of the strongest emotions we experience. Anger has a strong impact on the person who feels it, often dredging up feelings that distress us. Anger can have a strong effect on the people witnessing it, too, because of its potency and unpredictability. We often fear anger in ourselves and are uncomfortable with it in others. As parents, before we can focus on anger in our families, we need to be aware of the ways anger shows itself in us. Irritability, impatience, and frustration are all forms of anger. Critical interactions are anger based; annoyance is anger based. Anger is a broad emotion.

> *As parents, we need to be aware of the ways anger shows itself in us.*

God our Parent shares His wisdom about anger in the book of Proverbs, but much of what He says we already know in our hearts. He tells us that anger is the key ingredient in the soup of contention and strife, and that unchecked anger leads to many sins (Proverbs 29:22). And we know that. He tells us that harsh words stir up anger in others, while a gentle answer turns wrath away (Proverbs 15:1). Again, deep down we know that. Our Father warns us not to hang around an angry person because we might learn his ways and become ensnared in anger ourselves (Proverbs 22:24). That makes sense.

But when I read these words with the eyes of a parent, I feel greatly convicted. These same verses reveal that my harsh words stir up some of the ugly anger I see in my children. They tell me that I commit many sins when I let my anger control me. Most convicting, they tell me that my children are learning the ways of anger from me. Of all the things I want to teach my children, how to be angry is not one of them. Or is it? What if I could teach my children how to be angry but not sin—how to be angry gracefully?

My husband, Dick, recalls with regret one afternoon when God showed him a brief but powerful picture of what his anger looked like to his daughter. He and Anna Kate were getting ready to leave for Wednesday night church. In typical form, my daughter's pace did not suit my husband, and he impressed upon her the need to hurry. He instructed her to find her Bible, use the bathroom, put on her shoes, and find her coat—and then he left the room to get himself ready. Well, you know where this is going. The urgency that my husband felt so strongly did not register at all with our daughter.

As he gathered up his belongings, he put in his shirt pocket a little handheld recorder he planned to use to record some thoughts later that evening. When he returned to retrieve my daughter, she was far from ready. Apparently she had spent her time tying her shoelaces in multiple knots and still had yet to find her coat, use the bathroom, or get her Bible. My exasperated husband quickly helped Anna Kate to finish and get into the car, all the while "explaining" how important it was for her to concentrate, complete her tasks, and be on time. As it happened, he had inadvertently turned his recorder on and recorded his comments to Anna Kate.

When he realized this later, he listened to himself with pain and regret. He was shocked to hear this mean man talking so harshly to his beloved daughter. At the time he had felt that his exasperation was justified, and his comments reasonable and instructive. But the sharpness and accusation that colored each word were so out of proportion to her offense, so condemning. Yet he was even more dismayed at Anna Kate's reaction—or lack of it. Rather than become upset, she had seemed to take it in stride. Was she used to this kind of tirade? Had she become accustomed to such harshness? He later apologized to her and told her that he did not want to talk to her like that anymore.

I had a similar experience a few years ago as I caught a glimpse of myself in the mirror while reprimanding a child.

Not a pretty sight. But how can we get our point across to our children that their behavior is unacceptable if they don't see our anger? Is it ever acceptable to get angry and to show anger to a child?

When Love Gets Angry

To answer our questions, we look closely at the times when God has been angry with His children. While there are many, many passages we could study, let's focus on the passage in Matthew 23 that we refer to as the seven woes. Jesus is angry, and He's letting the Pharisees have it. But what looks at first like unbridled and unplanned anger, just what we are trying to avoid with our children, is in fact a clear picture of those few areas in which it is right and reasonable to get angry.

Jesus was angry because the Pharisees were not acting in innocent ignorance when they committed their sins, but rather covering their actions with pious religiosity. As religious leaders, they were working to get people converted, but then were tutoring people in selfishness rather than in the ways of God. They were leading their followers astray, taking advantage of their lack of knowledge. It made Jesus angry that, while they considered themselves righteous, they had no concept of the important virtues of justice, mercy, and faithfulness. He scolded them for working so hard to look good on the outside, all the while hiding the greed and self-indulgence that was on the inside. Essentially, Jesus was reprimanding them for being disobedient and for doing what was wrong *when they knew better,* all the while trying to appear righteous (Matthew 23:13–32). In our home, we call that sneaky defiance, and this is worthy of an angry response.

The difference between defiance and any other unwanted behavior in a child is that it is deliberate testing of the boundaries, rather than simply childish indiscretion. Sometimes children do this when the boundaries are not clear enough or when the rules in the home change without notice. Children will force you to set a clear and consistent boundary by breaking the rules in an obvious "I'm not gonna and you can't make me" way. This is behavior you can easily address.

But sneaky defiance is different. It's breaking the rules with the goal of getting away with something while still looking good. This behavior teaches children that it's okay to break the rules as long as you cover yourself and don't get caught. This is the behavior that so angers God—and therefore should so anger us—because it flies in the face of authenticity and integrity. Its goal is to look good on the outside with no concern for the issues of the heart. When our children act this way, they are more concerned with getting away with something than with the person they are becoming.

But before we parents begin confronting our children's sneaky defiance, we need to take a careful look at how we may be encouraging this behavior. Encouraging sneaky defiance? What self-respecting parent would do that? Well, frankly, you and I would. In a child's mind, if there is a great deal of emphasis put on what his family looks like—how it is behaving and how it presents itself to others—he can begin to think that this is more important than anything. If most of our emphasis in training our children is on their outward behavior, on their public achievements and appearance, then we are encouraging sneaky defiance.

If most of our emphasis in training our children is on their outward behavior, then we are encouraging sneaky defiance.

I know of far too many children who are beautiful, talented, and poised but who lack integrity. They know how to fly just under the behavior radar of their parents and school authorities. These are often the bullies and the ringleaders in the cliques that plague so many other children. They know how to command an audience of their peers with their negative behavior, but they have an intuitive sense of how to hide their behavior from adults. I worry about these children more than about those who are overtly defiant because they are harder to detect and therefore less likely to have their behavior addressed. The saddest part is that they often have parents who cannot—or will not—accept that their children are actually defying them. How difficult would it be for you to find that you have one of these children in your home?

In order to cultivate integrity in our children, we must consistently teach them that the state of one's heart is more important than outward appearance, that honesty and forthrightness about one's behavior is crucial. We need to hold them accountable each and every time they defy us—be it overt defiance or sneaky defiance.

But if we want our children to learn this or any other lesson regarding their behavior, we must keep away from disciplining them in our anger. Being angry at your children's behavior and disciplining them in anger are two different things. We human beings are made to shut down intellectually and emotionally in the face of strong negative emotion. It is a protective reflex, and it comes in handy from time to time. But if we are trying to teach our children something about their behavior or about our expectations of them as we are yelling at them, then we're wasting our breath. What's more, we're damaging our relationship with them. The connectedness of that relationship will do more to make you heard than the volume of your voice or the intensity of your anger.

PLANNING FOR ANGER

Most of the time we don't plan to get angry with our children; it just happens. It is an unplanned and often unpleasant event, and I usually don't react well to unpleasant events that take me by surprise.

When my children were little, they would often like to reenact funny or surprising moments over and over again, laughing uproariously each and every time. One day, I was making up my young son's bed, straightening the covers and fluffing the pillows, my mind a million miles away. Suddenly, a little hand reached out from under the bed and grabbed my ankle. My shock and resulting screams were hilarious to my son, who was laughing hysterically under the bed. Once the laughter subsided—both mine and his—he wanted to reenact the event over and over, rolling with laughter each time as if it were the first.

When he first surprised me, there is no way I could have prepared for it. I didn't expect it and so I was not in control of my reaction. But the second and third and fourth and fifth times he grabbed my ankle, I was prepared. Each time, I faked surprise and shock, but I planned my reactions.

If we are to take responsibility for our angry reactions, then we must *plan* to get angry. It's going to happen anyway, so we had better make a plan for when it does. Simply having a plan—any plan—for anger diffuses its negative impact because when we have a plan, we are not subject to operating out of our emotions.

> *If we are to take responsibility*
> *for our angry reactions, then we*
> *must plan to get angry.*

We all have different "trigger points" for what makes us angry at our children. Mine often center on my children doing things that embarrass me, not living up to their word or their potential, and being careless with the feelings of others. What are your trigger points? If you don't know what triggers your anger at your children, then you will be surprised by it again and again, each time resulting in an uncontrolled and unpleasant response that will wound rather than build up your relationship with that child.

Set some personal boundaries (see chapter 1) for when you are angry that are rigid enough to keep you from hurting anyone but wide enough to allow you to express honest emotion. You need to feel your anger, not simply respond robotically to it, so that you can discern what is behind the anger. Instead of using long explanations, I recommend that you use a parenting *sound bite*—a short, simple phrase that carries much meaning. For example, you may decide you're going to use the sound bite "I need a minute" to remove yourself from a heated argument so you can process your feelings and decide how you're going to respond.

When you and your spouse have a plan for getting angry, you set a family precedent for how your children may respond in their anger. You cannot mandate that your children not get angry. You can, however, set some guidelines for what is acceptable behavior *when* someone is angry. These guidelines will be effective if and only if you yourself have adopted them in your responses to anger. In other words, get the log out of your own eye before you look at the specks in your children's eyes (Matthew 7:5).

The following is a list of guidelines or boundaries you might choose to set as a family regarding behavior—everyone's behavior—during times of anger:

- any family member can call a five-minute time-out from heated discussion

- we will all try to use a controlled tone of voice when speaking

- we will show respect for each other by not interrupting

- we will try to stay away from blaming each other

- we will not use name-calling or attacks on a person's character

- family members may disagree, but no one may be disrespectful

In practice, these or any other boundaries will be a little messier. For example, anyone in the family can ask for a five-minute time-out during a heated discussion—even if the heat is on them. A child might at first try to use this to avoid some much-deserved pressure you're putting on him. However, once he realizes that the time-out lasts for only five minutes and then it's right back to the discussion, he's not so likely to call for one frivolously.

KEEPING THE BIGGER PICTURE IN MIND

Scripture tells us that our Father is "slow to anger, abounding in love and faithfulness" (Exodus 34:6). Notice it does not say that God doesn't get angry. We see in Scripture over and over again the wrath of God against His people and their rebelliousness. God's anger is (or should be) scary and mysterious to us, just as our anger is to our children. However, there is an important distinction between our anger at others and God's anger toward us. God the Parent never forgets the bigger plan, the greater truth, about Himself and His children, even in anger. He knows all too well the countless cycles of rebellion and repentance that His people run through. You can set your historical watch by it. But in these endless cycles, God keeps His loving eye on the bigger plan—the redemption and sanctification (the growing up) of His children, with whom He is in utter and unexplainable love.

The key to these cycles, though, is love—specifically God's

love for us, even when He's angry. His definition of love found in 1 Corinthians 13 is familiar to many of us:

> Love is patient, love is kind. It does not envy, it does not boast, it is not proud. It is not rude, it is not self-seeking, it is not easily angered, it keeps no record of wrongs. (1 Corinthians 13:4–5)

Did you notice that it didn't say, "Love never gets angry"? It said that love "is not easily angered." There's a difference. And that's followed by another very important piece—love "keeps no record of wrongs," something I find hard to avoid when I'm angry with someone. These verses show us that when we love someone we will occasionally get angry with them, but we still have a choice between acting in love or acting in selfishness. Acting in selfishness always leads to more anger and more resentment, while acting in love and refusing to hang on to resentment leads to deeper love.

When we love someone we will occasionally get angry with them, but we still have a choice between acting in love or acting in selfishness.

Just as God does with us, we must also keep in mind the bigger process that our children are moving through—the process of growing up. And growing up is messy. No matter how well we parent, growing up just doesn't follow any straight and organized plan. Our children learn and grow primarily by making mistakes and getting up and trying again. But how likely are our children to do the *get up and try it again* part if our response to their mistakes is swift and angry?

TALKING ABOUT ANGER

As we begin to deal with the anger that erupts from our hearts toward our children, we realize that they, too, struggle with anger at times. Parents are usually uncomfortable when witnessing outbursts of anger from their children. Because they are children, they will be less in control of their behavior and less apt to hide their anger. This can be both good and bad. Outbursts of anger can be upsetting, but they are much easier to deal with than are the seeds of bitterness that take root when we don't even know they are there.

Just as God our Parent encourages us to do in Proverbs, we must teach our children how to stay in control of their anger. This is closely tied with teaching them to be in control of what they say, because often what is said in anger is harmful. We want to train a child to respond in a healthy way to his anger. However, this will never be accomplished by meeting his anger with our anger.

In helping a child to learn from an angry experience, it is important to first treat his anger like a third party. In other words, see him as separate from his anger, so when you interact with him you can do so in a cooperative shoulder-to-shoulder approach rather than a confrontational face-to-face encounter. When someone is angry, a face-to-face encounter will without fail lead to more anger, either spoken (shouting or arguing) or unspoken (resentfulness and bitterness).

If your child is clearly angry, you can speak about the anger as a separate entity from the child by saying, "Don't let your anger get control of you," or "Your anger is starting to control you, so you need to take a deep breath." This way the approach is not "me against you and your anger" (face-to-face), but rather "me and you against your anger" (shoulder-to-shoulder).

After an angry episode, you can look together at the ways your child let his anger get control of him and the ways he took control of his anger. If your child did not do a good job of taking responsibility for his anger, there may need to be consequences. Even so, he is not bearing the consequences *for getting angry* but for failing to take responsibility for his anger.

Anger can be a confusing and paralyzing emotion, so it is important that you reconnect with your child after an angry exchange. This may involve an exchange of apologies. It's important for your child to apologize for his behavior, and it's important that you apologize as well if you have let your anger control you in some way. Not only is this simply the right thing to do, but it also models for your child the importance of asking for and receiving forgiveness. In this intimate time of reconciliation, you get to love each other, fully aware of your mutual frailties as human beings.

Consider This...

- In what kinds of situations do you find yourself getting angry with your children? Try to be specific. Do you believe that the methods you're using to communicate with your children when you're angry are working? Is there evidence of this? Ask them if they agree.

- What benefits do you see in maintaining a controlled tone when talking with your children? How hard will this be for you? What is your plan to ensure that you will keep a stable, matter-of-fact tone of voice during an angry confrontation with one of your children?

- What are some boundaries you feel you can set in your home regarding the way anger is handled? Be specific and try to think of at least five.

- How have you dealt with your children when they were angry? Would you consider this a shoulder-to-shoulder or a face-to-face approach? What are some ways you can talk to your child about his anger that separates his anger from him as a person?

Chapter Seven

WITH MY
WHOLE HEART

Both of my children have strong personalities. (I can't imagine *where* they got them!) When they have an opinion, a belief, or a commitment, they throw themselves wholeheartedly into it. They feel strongly—sometimes about important life issues, but usually about pursuits that cause my husband and me to shake our heads in disbelief. Take, for instance, the gum wrapper collection my daughter is so committed to. She spends her allowance on gum so she can chew it and collect the wrappers and then take the wrappers to the recycling station for cash. What a great idea! We figure she will need to spend roughly $102,000 on gum to have enough wrappers to get back thirty-seven cents from recycling. But she's devoted to the cause!

People devote themselves to literally thousands of pursuits and people, causes and pastimes, over the course of our lives. We are devoted to our spouses, our work, and our children. We can also devote ourselves to lesser pursuits such as a football team, a hobby, or a collection. Devotion makes us do things we never thought we could or would. Those bare-chested men who paint their overweight bodies with the colors of their favorite football team and spell out profound messages such as "Go Titans!" are devoted to their cause. But those students who lost their lives in Tiananmen Square protesting the civil rights atrocities in Beijing in 1989, we also call devoted.

> **Devotion makes us do things we never thought we could or would.**

True devotion is more than simply being committed to something or someone; it is a profound dedication or attachment, taking precedence over other commitments. Devotion remains firm and does not wax and wane with the circumstances. Devotion usually increases with time but does not depend upon good times alone for its growth. You can choose to be devoted to another person, a cause, a project, or a belief, but your devotion to God Himself is the one that colors all others.

INEXPLICABLE DEVOTION

My daughter, Anna Kate, has a little sister named Molly. Well, actually, Molly is an American Girl doll who was adopted by our family when Anna Kate was five. Since the day she received Molly, my daughter has loved her with a devotion that is curious to my husband and me. The Sunday school teachers are always confused when Anna Kate draws a picture of our family that includes her little sister Molly, since they are pretty sure she only has an older brother. Molly must be kissed good night or she gets her feelings hurt. Molly has an extensive wardrobe and receives presents at Christmas. Because Anna Kate is devoted to Molly, we are all devoted to Molly.

In some ways Anna Kate's devotion to Molly doesn't really make sense. But then, genuine devotion rarely makes sense. Anna Kate doesn't love Molly because of what Molly can do; she loves her because she is her "sister." In the same way, we love Anna Kate not because of what she can do, but because she is our daughter. Our devotion to her defies reason at times. But do you know why we can love her like this, even when she tests the limits of our love? "We love because [God] first loved us" (1 John 4:19); we are devoted because He was first devoted to us.

God's devotion to his children—His wayward, unfaithful, wishy-washy children—defies reason. How many times, I wonder, has He wanted to rid this beautiful planet of the rebellious and stubborn bunch of knuckleheads He calls His children? I am thankful He is not swayed in His love for me when I act in a manner unworthy of my position as His child, when I willingly break my devotion to Him. Over and over again God says to His children, "You are mine and I am not leaving!" He makes a covenant with us and sticks to it. He may use our circumstances to give us a divine time-out or even a divine spanking, but He does not forfeit His parental responsibility nor abandon His love for us no matter how impossibly we behave. When I allow the full depth of my sin and selfishness to sink in, and then see it in light of God's unwavering devotion to me, I am speechless.

From the first bud of springtime to the cry of a newborn baby, God renews His commitment to us over and over. He knows we will occasionally forget we are His children if He doesn't remind us constantly. As the Israelites, our forefathers in the faith, wandered and whined in the wilderness, God had to keep assuring them of His commitment to His family. Standing on the banks of the Red Sea, the Egyptian army in hot pursuit, the newly freed Israelites did what you and I are apt to do. They forgot. Even though they had seen with their own eyes the undeniable power of God in the plagues on Egypt, they were children, and they forgot. They forgot that God was not only their God, He was their Father. They forgot that God would not lead them out of oppression in Egypt just to let them die at the hands of those same oppressors. They forgot—as you and I often do—that God was inexplicably and wholly devoted to them.

> *The Israelites forgot—as you and*
> *I often do—that God was inexplicably*
> *and wholly devoted to them.*

In the face of such strong and undeserved love, what is our response? As our children often do to us, we take the love of the Father for granted. When we do, however, we miss so much. We miss the magnitude and the beauty of a life lived outside of ourselves, serving a God we will never fully understand. We miss the keen awareness of each other that we enjoy when we are not focused so wholly on our own circumstances. When our life is lived in response to God's devotion to us and not simply in what He can give us or do for us, we enjoy a richer and more tangible faith for which there is no substitute.

Devotion to God is not merely a Sunday school lesson; it is a way of life, and our children need to see it as such. In our faith-walk, our children get a rare chance to see us be brave and noble, unwavering in our resolve to obey. In faith they see us boldly live out the promises of God, fully believing that He has our highest and best interests at heart. Like many of you, my husband and I long to see our children grow in faith. We want more than anything for nobility and honor, trust and integrity to win their hearts, even as they are bombarded with opportunities for self-indulgence and immorality. Their only hope for developing this kind of lifestyle is in devoting themselves fully to God. But we know that nothing we say to our children about a life of faith will be taken seriously, unless we are transparent in our own devotion to God, in our loyalty to Him regardless of our circumstances, and in our dogged belief that He is who He says He is.

Devotion in Turn

A natural response to God's devotion to us is our devotion, in turn, to our children. God sees glimmers of Himself in us as we lovingly care for the children He has entrusted to us. This surely makes Him smile.

But parenting with devotion does not always look like a Hallmark moment. In His devotion, God loves me enough to make me bear the consequences of my actions, to reprimand me when I need to be brought back to reality, and to remind me on occasion that there is a God and I am not He. In short, My Father is devoted to growing me up. We must be devoted to our children in the same way—devoted to parenting them in the awkward evolution we call growing up.

Children need to know that you are committed to them.

They need the security that comes with knowing that you are never going to stop loving them. This confidence is shaken regularly. It is not unusual for a young child who has just been punished to wonder if his mom and dad still love him. Perhaps the most damaging to this sense of security is when a child's parents argue or fight in his presence. He may think, "If my parents can stop loving each other, then can they stop loving me, too?"

As children become teenagers and develop wills of their own, they are more often in conflict with their parents. This is a natural and even healthy phase of growing up, even though it can strain the parent-child relationship for a time. During this period our devotion should not take the form of giving in to our children nor of adopting an authoritarian role. Instead, we set and enforce important boundaries for them, we encourage them in their pursuits, and we maintain a fierce devotion to them regardless of their choices.

I once knew a family whose father held a prominent position in the community. When the children were young, they were obedient, bright, and thoughtful. As the oldest son became a teenager, however, their family began to look a little more "real." Like his father, the son had a will of his own—with orange and green hair to match! In an exasperated moment, his father once said to me, "I've just given up on him. I don't know what else to do. I give up." I reminded him that he did not have that option. None of us has that option.

When we are in conflict with our children on any level, we have a unique opportunity to model for them the devotion of the Father. God loves us no matter what, and so we have the power to love our children *no matter what.*

*When we are in conflict with our children,
we have a unique opportunity to model for
them the devotion of the Father.*

TENDING THE HEART OF A CHILD

We parents need to be sure we are saying aloud what we know in our hearts to help our children learn about the beauty and complexity of devotion to the Father. As we talk to our children about God, we must be sure to tell them *how* He shows Himself to be a devoted Parent to us and to them, how He is committed to His children regardless of our behavior. They need to hear that "neither death nor life, neither angels nor demons, neither the present nor the future, nor any powers, neither height nor depth, nor anything else in all creation, will be able to separate us from the love of God" (Romans 8:38–39).

Many parents assume this is what they are communicating to their children by the way they live, but children are much more concrete than this. They need to be told, and told often. We must talk about these and all things pertaining to God as we live our lives day to day. God teaches us to talk about His truths to our children, "talking about them when you sit at home and when you walk along the road, when you lie down and when you get up" (Deuteronomy 11:19).

Children need an illustration of an abstract concept like devotion. I often suggest to parents that they read a classic novel together as a family, regardless of the ages of their children.

Using literature as a springboard, the family can talk about all sorts of concepts, including devotion. Almost every child's chapter book describes a character devoted to some process or person. Fern is devoted to caring for Wilbur in *Charlotte's Web*, and the spider Charlotte devotes herself to saving Wilbur from the slaughterhouse. In *The Secret Garden*, Mary and Colin devote themselves to restoring the neglected garden. And perhaps most strikingly, the lion Aslan in *The Lion, the Witch and the Wardrobe* devotes himself to four children, even to the point of giving his life to spare the rebellious Edmund.

While we cannot mandate that a child be devoted to something—for this is a matter of the heart—we can train and nurture the concept of devotion from a very young age. When discussing devotion with our children, we might simply use the word as we talk about the pursuits and people they are committed to. "Wow, you're really devoted to your piano playing, aren't you?" "You really showed yourself to be a devoted friend when you _____." "Your teacher must really be devoted to her class if she spent all that time _____." Help your children initially to see devotion as a virtuous commitment. Later they can be taught the full breadth of the beauty of devotion.

We train in our children an appreciation for devotion and even the ability to be devoted to something when we hold them accountable to the commitments they have made. We never allow them to quit a team they have joined unless it is somehow damaging to them. Even if they are injured and cannot participate, they can sit on the bench, cheering their teammates. Once they have committed to a musical instrument, we train devotion by holding them accountable to practice whether they feel like it or not. If they have been invited to a friend's house and then receive a better offer, they must keep their commitment to the friend they initially promised their time to.

We train in our children an appreciation for devotion when we hold them accountable to the commitments they have made.

DEVOTION TO ONE ANOTHER

Growing up, my siblings and I had a hard time loving each other. There were four of us, and we drove everybody, including each other, crazy. I would have just as soon sold my two younger sisters to the gypsies as look at them, but if someone outside of our family insulted or ridiculed them in any way, I jumped to their defense. My devotion to them seemed nonexistent when we were together, but at the core, we loved and were devoted to one another. So it is with many siblings during the growing-up years.

How much richer our childhood could have been if my siblings and I had been devoted to one another in brotherly love (Romans 12:10). As we seek to teach our children about being committed to one another, we need to define what that means for them as siblings. Being devoted to each other does not entail taking on a sugary sweet, artificial tone when together. But devotion does mean loving each other in such a way that no one has to be first or right or in charge all the time.

Parents sometimes resign themselves too easily to the inevitability of sibling rivalry. Yes, it is normal for siblings to disagree, even to argue and fight. Nevertheless, we can require some degree of civility and kindness from our children toward each other. In doing so, we show them what it means to be devoted to someone even when angry or annoyed with them. We need to give them the vision that they will be family for the rest of their lives and that their devotion to one another is important and lasting.

Above and Beyond the Call of Duty

In our society, we like to keep our options open. We like to have choices about how we spend our time, our money, and our attention. Being obligated to someone or to a task feels constricting, and so we may avoid committing ourselves. And yet we admire people who are devoted to a cause or a task, such as those who fulfill their duty to their country by serving in the armed forces. As adults we are duty-bound in many areas. We have a duty to pay our taxes, to obey the laws, to provide for our families. At any given time, we can choose to shirk our responsibilities, and sometimes we do.

Devotion is a higher calling than simply doing one's duty. The difference between duty and devotion lies in the motivation behind it. We feel obligated to perform a duty; we feel compelled to devote ourselves. Duty is fulfilling the contract—no less than I promised, but not a whit more. Devotion is giving whatever it takes and not waiting for the warm, fuzzy feelings to kick in. There is an element of emotion that compels us to give ourselves fully to the object of our devotion, be it a task or a person. At the same time, my devotion is not swayed by a lack of emotion or even by negative emotion. I am devoted *no matter what*, even when it's not fun, even when it doesn't feel good.

It's easy to be kind to others when they are kind to you, but to be respectful of someone who is acting unkind requires devotion. This may be devotion to a person, as in a marriage when your devotion to the relationship overrides (usually) your desire to be unkind. In other circumstances, the devotion is to God, who calls you to love those who hate you (Matthew 5:43–45). Whatever the case, there will be evidence of your devotion. It is unreasonable for us to claim we are devoted to something when there is no evidence of it. It is important for our children to understand that there is no casual devotion, no easy road to giving oneself wholeheartedly.

> *There is no casual devotion, no easy*
> *road to giving oneself wholeheartedly.*

DIVIDED DEVOTION

When he's writing to the church in Corinth, Paul encourages the believers there to live "in undivided devotion to the Lord" (1 Corinthians 7:35). He challenges them to a life of concentrated, unadulterated commitment. This is the kind of commitment we want to have not only in our personal relationship with God but also in those pursuits God calls us to—not the least of which is parenting.

There are several ways we can be divided in our devotion as parents. First, and probably most common, we can easily overcommit our time to the multitude of worthy causes vying for our attention outside of the home: Bible studies, work opportunities, charities, volunteer work, school duties, fundraisers, church work, mission work—the list is endless. It's tempting to commit to pursuits such as these because the rewards of gratitude and praise may be a pleasant contrast to the seemingly thankless job of being a parent.

I have struggled to be undivided in my commitment to my children as I see so many places that "need" me. Countless times in my life I've said "yes" to commitments to which I should have said a resounding "*no!*" Sometimes I regret a commitment the minute I make it, foreseeing (a minute too late) the effect it will have on my family. Yet, as we look at each and every snapshot in the Scriptures of God the Parent in action, we never see Him distracted from His single-minded devotion to the task of growing His children up.

Certainly parents must juggle responsibilities. We have to budget our time and balance everyone's schedules. But if we are willing to look at our commitments with an open heart, we likely will see some we are not called to and that actually keep us from focusing on our primary responsibility of parenting. On occasion I force myself to open my date book to the Lord and ask Him which commitments were a mistake. Sometimes He has to give me the courage—because I don't have it in myself—to apologize and ask to be released from those commitments.

Another way that we may be divided in our devotion occurs, ironically, in our efforts to be good parents. We read every new parenting book that comes out, we participate in parent workshops, we host Bible studies for parents, we attend Sunday school classes geared for parents. In this pursuit of the perfect solutions to all our family woes, we can easily be tossed to and fro by every new parenting idea and philosophy that comes along. Every time you start a new program or incorporate a new recommended tactic into your parenting arsenal, you run the risk of blindly subscribing to someone else's notion of good parenting. This someone else doesn't know your children, and he doesn't know you. Be careful not to take the easy road of simply adopting someone else's agenda for your children—simply recycling someone else's parenting. Pursue God. Hear from Him. Ask Him for the wisdom that He gives so generously without reproach (James 1:5). I write this, of course, with keen awareness that right now you are reading this parenting book. What I hope you will learn, however, is not yet another set of parenting tips or tactics, but how to pursue your Parent and how to enlist the help and expertise of the One who parents you.

Devotion is a deep love and commitment. It requires great dedication and loyalty. It encompasses strong enthusiasm and admiration. It is love. It takes a lot of energy to be devoted to something or to someone, yet devotion can release energy in us as well. As difficult as it can be, we were made to be devoted.

We are devoted to the Giver, not to His gifts.
We must never confuse the two.

True devotion requires commitment that oftentimes defies reason. We are devoted to God whether He makes us prosper or not, because His blessings are not required for our devotion. We are devoted to the Giver, not to His gifts. We must never confuse the two. The prophet Habakkuk knew this distinction well:

Though the fig tree does not bud
and there are no grapes on the vines,
though the olive crop fails
and the fields produce no food,
though there are no sheep in the pen
and no cattle in the stalls,
yet I will rejoice in the LORD,
I will be joyful in God my Savior
(Habakkuk 3:17–18).

- Based on what is in your daily calendar, in your checkbook register, and on your mind, to what are you devoted? To what is your family devoted—not in theory, but in practice?

- In 1 Corinthians 7:35, Paul encourages the Corinthians to live "in undivided devotion to the Lord." How might you be divided in your devotion to His calling on you as a parent? What are some possible remedies for this situation?

- Think of a time when your children had the opportunity to witness your devotion or faithfulness to the Father despite your circumstances. Describe that time. What was communicated to your children? If you cannot think of one, look for opportunities this week to communicate to your children something of your personal devotion to God.

- Think of a time when your children had the opportunity to witness you remaining devoted to *them* despite the circumstances. Describe that time. Ask your children to describe that time. Is what you meant to be communicated what was actually communicated?

Chapter Eight

GROWING THROUGH DISAPPOINTMENT

When Claire was a precocious three-year-old, speaking in complete and eloquent sentences and growing bored with traditional toddler toys, her proud parents were certain she was gifted. She read fluently at four and wrote imaginative stories at five, and they began to talk about her entering school early, skipping grades, and perhaps placing her in a special program for gifted children. Now in the fourth grade, ten-year-old Claire is clearly bright; however, recent testing has shown that she is not intellectually gifted. She does well in school but lacks the extraordinary ingenuity and creativity that characterize gifted students. As I shared these findings with her parents, their disappointment was obvious.

They asked the questions parents ask when they do not agree with the test results—"How valid are these tests, really?" and "She didn't feel well that morning, so wouldn't that affect her score?" I understood their disappointment. Their plans for her future—high school valedictorian, top SAT scores, an academic scholarship—were thwarted by this news. But it was more than this. They still loved her, of course, but the vision they held of their daughter, their hopes and dreams for her, were all tinged with the idea that she was intellectually gifted.

No one likes to be disappointed, to have things turn out differently than we planned or hoped, to not get our way. Prior to any disappointment, there must be an expectation, an agenda, a notion of something that we believe will, or at least should, happen. And our experience confirms that the disappointment we feel will always be as strong as the expectation behind it.

> *No one likes to be disappointed,*
> *to have things turn out differently*
> *than we planned or hoped.*

DISAPPOINTMENT AS TEACHER

Scripture illustrates that God's children have experienced plenty of disappointment and that their Father wisely made use of those circumstances to teach and train His children. For example, Joshua was chosen to lead the Israelites with the strength and devotion of Moses before him. God confirmed the appointment by granting Joshua a glorious victory in the capture of Jericho. After the big win, the Israelites were flying high (Joshua 6).

Joshua sent his army confidently into battle for an easy victory against the town of Ai. To everyone's great surprise, they lost. They didn't just lose, they were whipped, routed, devastated. When the news of defeat reached camp, the Scriptures say that "the hearts of the people melted and became like water" (Joshua 7:5). Did God stand between His children and disappointment? Did He sympathize with His people and tell them "we'll get 'em next time"? No. He had in mind the bigger picture of growing His children up. God used the disappointment of their defeat to teach Joshua and the people of Israel to obey Him. In the following years, the Israelites' disobedience and childishness provided more opportunities for God to discipline and teach, and He used these just as effectively. He does the same with us.

Often God allows and uses disappointing circumstances to cause us to pull back and take a more careful look at how we are living. But for us parents, it can be a heartbreaking and painful experience to witness our child suffering through disappointment. We mothers especially can whip out our bear claws when the happiness of one of our cubs is threatened. However, we need to resist the temptation to intervene, to arrange our children's worlds so that they are never disappointed, and so rob them of one of life's most effective learning experiences. Plans fall through, friends betray, hoped-for awards go to others. We want to soften the blow by avoiding the truth, by offering distractions, by making excuses, but in doing so we prevent the experience of disappointment from having its beneficial effect.

As children of God in a disappointing world, we know that disappointment can be a stark reminder that we are not in control of this life—and that we ought not be. Sometimes disappointment requires us to find another way to accomplish a task, to meet a goal, or to consider a relationship. The struggle helps us grow. The same is true for our children. So if we stand in the way of their disappointing experiences, we are likely standing in the way of their growth and maturity. Through struggle and disappointment, our children develop such traits as tenacity, resilience, and commitment. When they must "try, try again," they cultivate perseverance and hope. A child's character is so much more important than the satisfaction of getting what he wanted in the first place.

> *If we stand in the way of our children's disappointing experiences, we are likely standing in the way of their growth and maturity.*

On the other hand, we shouldn't simply step aside and watch our children be overwhelmed by disappointment. As you walk with your children through disappointments, keep an eye out for debilitating patterns. If a child repeatedly finds himself in situations that disappoint, he stands a good chance of becoming embittered. Instead of it being a learning experience, the situation may be calling for a change to be made. For example, if a child is consistently disappointed by his failing grades, even as he gives faithful effort, something needs to change. Perhaps he needs a tutor or more time with the teacher. Perhaps the school setting or level of expectation needs adjusting. Whatever the case may be, if we do not respond to his constant disappointment, he is likely to become bitter and pessimistic. He may stop trying altogether and slip into a passive-aggressive style in which he protects himself by refusing to try or even to participate. In these cases too, we parent our children by helping them to see God's truth in the midst of the disappointment.

Walking Through Disappointment

Sarah, an only child, was struggling to keep friends in her second-grade class. She made friends, but she couldn't seem to keep them. Her impulsive and sometimes rude comments to classmates had hurt many feelings and made other children think twice before inviting Sarah to play. When Sarah's mother found out about a classmate's birthday party that Sarah was not invited to, her heart broke for her daughter. Her initial reaction was disbelief—"There must be some mistake"—and then, realizing there was no mistake, anger. She wanted to protect Sarah from hurtful disappointment and tried to keep the party a secret. She planned to do something fun and exciting with Sarah on the day of the party to make up for her being left out. She even dreamed of wonderful ideas for Sarah's next birthday party—to which the other little girl would *not* be invited!

Who among us would not go to the same places of anger and even revenge when one of our children is faced with such disappointment? Our natural reaction to anyone hurting or rejecting our child is to protect—sometimes with a vengeance! But this mother's reaction robbed her of a chance to learn a greater truth about her daughter, and to offer better help to Sarah than simply planning her next birthday party. Sarah's impulsiveness and rudeness toward her friends was at the root of her social problem. Not being invited to the birthday party was a natural consequence, a symptom of the problem. The disappointment of not being invited, while painful, had great potential to help Sarah in her development as a person. Learning to be a good friend was a more pressing need than avoiding disappointment.

Our job as parents is to counter the chance that bitterness will set in by simply walking in truthful love with our children through their disappointing experiences, keeping our eyes open to the possible changes that need to be made. This does not mean frantically running through a checklist of suggestions until we find one that works. Nor is it wise for us to maneuver behind the scenes, righting every wrong suffered by our children. They learn best when we simply and matter-of-factly accompany them through difficult times with confidence in God's greater plans, remembering that disappointment can be a door to growth and development.

Helping our children put words to their feelings and thoughts is a practical first step. Often children have difficulty talking about their feelings because they do not have the vocabulary to express their thoughts. Even with children as young as three years, it is extremely important to acknowledge their disappointment, to place labels on the anger or resentment or sadness they might be feeling. We should never try to dictate their feelings by telling them what to feel, but we can help them talk about those feelings safely and honestly.

It is extremely important to acknowledge our children's disappointment, to place labels on the anger or resentment or sadness they might be feeling.

We must be careful not to dismiss our child's disappointment even if it seems unfounded or trivial; when we acknowledge her feelings we build our relationship with her.

God's love for us teaches us to cherish and nurture relationships beyond all else. When the tender heart of a child is hurt, no matter what the reason, we have a unique opportunity to help her grow while strengthening our relationship with her. In the same way, when we are confronted by life's disappointments, we can seek out our Parent, and our relationship will be nurtured as we invite Him to walk with us through disappointing times.

Because it can go unnoticed, it is important to discern what a child may think the disappointing experience says about him as a person. What messages have made their home in his heart? Sometimes a disappointing event will leave a child feeling stupid or unpopular, incapable or even unlovable—impressions that can be strong and lasting. When they are not verbalized, these impressions become indelibly stamped in our children's hearts and minds. When we help our children speak the messages aloud without fear of judgment, we have a chance to affirm or challenge each one, weakening the power held by messages hidden inside.

Only after the emotional sting of the disappointing experience has worn off a bit is our child ready to hear the deeper truth that God may be teaching him. We may help him to explore aloud some different ways to approach similar situations in the future. He needs to hear us speak with empathy ("I understand") instead of with sympathy ("Oh, you poor thing"). Our matter-of-fact frankness about the events helps children see beyond the emotion that each event generated, to the truth God has for them. The Bible calls this speaking the truth in love, and our heavenly Parent always speaks the truth in love to His children.

Disappointment in Others

There is a significant difference between being disappointed that events didn't turn out the way we had planned, and being disappointed in a particular person. I saw that clearly when a recent playdate for my daughter fell through. That morning, Anna Kate had invited her friend to visit, and she was coming over around lunchtime. Twelve o'clock came and went. Then one o'clock. By two o'clock we called and found out that her friend had gone to the mall with another friend. While Anna Kate was disappointed her plans fell through, the real sting was in the apparent betrayal of her friend. She was irritated that she didn't have a playdate that afternoon, but she felt wounded by what her friend had done to her.

Once the steam of my own anger had cleared, I realized why Anna Kate was so disappointed. We are disappointed only in those we love, care for, or trust. We have few expectations of those we don't care about or trust. She cared for her friend and trusted her. This made the sting of disappointment hurt even more.

When any disappointment in another remains unresolved, it follows a natural course and soon becomes resentment. It is one thing to be disappointed in someone; it is quite another to resent them. Even though resentment is born from disappointment, resentment includes a measure of bitterness that attaches to the person rather than the person's actions, enduring far beyond the initial pain of the disappointment. When my daughter saw her friend at school the next week, she still carried some of the sting of resentment.

Disappointment is one of our strongest teachers. Something this universal to all human experience must hold some rich spiritual lessons. Sometimes disappointment in a person reveals the unfair expectations we hold for others and for ourselves. At the root of any unreasonable expectation is selfishness; we are looking to others to fulfill us in some way, to make us feel good, to make us proud. How often we look to our children and to our spouses to complete and satisfy us in a way that only the Father can. This always leads to disappointment. An unrealized hope in another person serves to remind us that people are not able—were never in fact designed—to fully meet each other's needs. That is Someone else's job. We are bound to be disappointed when we carry such unrealistic expectations of each other.

> **We are bound to be disappointed when we carry unrealistic expectations of each other.**

Our children have faced disappointment practically from birth, starting with the first delayed diaper change or late feeding. It's simply part of life. However, it is important to remember that our children are driven by emotion and impulse, so they will go fairly quickly from disappointment to resentment. Simplistic in their thinking, they tend to believe that if someone disappoints them, they did so on purpose. When situations do not turn out as planned, they look for someone to blame—their friends, their parents, or God Himself. Without thought or discussion, a disappointing experience can easily turn into resentment. Therefore, we help our children when we talk with them about their disappointments, and when we model for them a healthy and mature response to the experience. This requires, of course, that we parents respond to disappointments in a healthy and mature way, and that we recognize and admit it when we don't.

FORGIVENESS

When our children's disappointment is in another person, we have a beautiful opportunity to walk our children through the difficult process of forgiveness. You know the dance—I want to forgive, but I don't want to; I hang on to my bitterness, but I long to be free of it; I want to give it to God, but I want to clutch it tightly. It's a neverending dance until we decide, as an act of our will, to forgive.

Adults and children alike have many misconceptions about the act of forgiveness. We often believe the other person has to first say she's sorry—or at least express sorrow—before she deserves forgiveness. God our Father puts this notion to rest in one verse. *The Message* says it like this: "Forgive one another as quickly and thoroughly as God in Christ forgave you" (Ephesians 4:32). Even though children have only an emerging sense of their own sin and the sacrifice Christ made to take care of that sin, they can understand forgiveness as an act of the will. We forgive because we choose to forgive, no matter what the other person does. And this is our heritage, because God chose to forgive us even when we didn't deserve it (Romans 5:8).

As our children walk through the forgiveness process, they are likely to want a response from the other person. If my child was wronged in some way (as in the case of the missing play-date), it may be appropriate for her to call the offender and simply state that her feelings were hurt but that she forgives her. Some children cannot bring themselves to confront another child in that way; for other children, that's the easy part. Either way, our child may find that the offender either doesn't know she has offended or doesn't care.

A child needs to see that it is not the response of the other person that heals her heart; it is Jesus who heals her heart. Her sense of closure, of peace, must not rely on the response of the one she forgives or she will be at the mercy of other people's responses. Her peace comes from knowing that she did the right thing even if the other person chose to do the wrong thing. Her peace comes from releasing the hurt and letting go of her expectation of how the other person should respond. Her peace comes from the relationship she enjoys with her Father and not from the other person.

DISAPPOINTMENT IN OUR CHILDREN

I have worked with many parents, especially of teenage and older children, who are disappointed in their children. Of course, any child is going to flub a test on occasion or forget to take out the trash; here I am referring to more significant issues. Perhaps the parents believe that the child does not achieve in school as his IQ indicates he should. Maybe a parent envisioned an Ivy League college for his daughter and instead she chooses the state university. Many parents are disappointed in their children's choices of friends, their selection of a mate, their style of dress, their extracurricular activities (or lack thereof).

More than a few of us live with a sense of injury from the way our children have let us down, how they fall short of their potential. It's easy to interpret this as intentional disregard for all we've done for them. When we are disappointed in our children's choices, we must guard our hearts against allowing that disappointment to turn into a sense of personal injury. In C. S. Lewis's *The Screwtape Letters*, Senior Devil Screwtape teaches Junior Devil Wormwood how people's disappointment can be used to pull them away from each other and even from God. Screwtape teaches Wormwood, "Whatever men expect they soon come to think they have a right to: the sense of disappointment can, with very little skill on our part, be turned into a sense of injury."

> *When we are disappointed in our children's choices, we must guard our hearts against allowing that disappointment to turn into a sense of personal injury.*

We must not forget, however, that the root of this disappointment is not only our children's behavior but also our expectations of them. Our hopes for our children are bound to disappoint us unless they are rooted in God's perspective and in our trust in Him.

We parents are rarely successful in concealing our disappointment. We reveal it by becoming easily exasperated. Exasperation is a close cousin to condemnation, with that sense of personal injury thrown in. When we are exasperated with our children, we communicate regularly that they don't measure up, that they disappoint us. We are in essence condemning them. Sadly, the fruit of our exasperation is perfectionism, then cynical pessimism, and finally rebellion.

This is obviously contrary to the deepest desires we hold for our children. We seek instead to inspire them to want better of themselves, to *expect* better of themselves. This requires us to lay aside our feelings and to keep our eyes on the goal of training our children through their mistakes—just as God our Parent does with us when we disappoint Him.

At one time or another, probably all parents feel disappointed in some aspect of their children's behavior, attitude, or choices. Some portion of this disappointment reflects our reasonable expectations of them. Other times our disappointment results from unfair and unreasonable expectations. Yet even when our expectations are right and reasonable, it is essential that we keep the disappointment in perspective—in perspective of God's higher plan, His sovereignty, and His desires for our children. Perhaps the very thing that disappoints us is exactly what God will use to teach both our children and us a stronger reliance on Him.

When We Disappoint

Just as with the Israelites, it is so easy to find ourselves with displaced priorities. Though we intend to focus the necessary attention on our children and families, we often find ourselves overscheduled, overworked, and overextended. This is disappointing to everyone involved. We disappoint our children when we neglect to be present and engaged with them, choosing instead to give our time to what seems to be a higher calling—building a business or career, taking a leadership role at church, helping others in need, keeping a beautiful home. The truth is there is no higher calling on us parents than to model God the Father before the children He has entrusted to us. The relationships we build with our children and the service we do as a family make up the legacy of love we will to pass to our children, but we must be intentional and faithful if we are to succeed in this high calling.

When I realize that I have not been the parent I needed to be in a particular situation, I experience a range of emotions. Feelings of guilt mixed with sorrow give me a strong desire to make things right. Here is where I can easily fall into the trap of guilt-reacting. Instead of acting in genuine love for my children, I may be tempted to act to soothe my guilt. I may pretend that I didn't really do anything wrong, and my children's disappointment is more about their selfishness than about me. Or I may offer a trip to McDonald's or a new DVD instead of asking for forgiveness and seeking to restore our relationship.

If we scramble to make up for our shortcomings when we disappoint our children, we miss a unique opportunity to show them that we can respond in a healthy way to being disappointed in ourselves. When they behave in a disappointing manner, we want them to recognize their error, ask for forgiveness, and seek to restore any relationships that may have been broken. Likewise, this is what we parents should do when we have acted in a disappointing way. Rather than placating and distracting my children from my misbehavior, I can acknowledge my error, ask for forgiveness, and get back to enjoying our relationships.

THE HOPE THAT DOES NOT DISAPPOINT

The most profound truth to emerge from a disappointing experience is the truth of our desperate need for a Savior. This is the central truth we need to learn about all of life's disappointments—and the truth we need to communicate to our children. The only expectation, the only hope that does not disappoint is the one we hold in God our Parent (Romans 5:5). Jesus will not disappoint us, and He will not disappoint our children. This is true not because He's committed to fulfilling our every wish and expectation. Rather, He does not disappoint because all our choicest wishes pale in comparison to Him; our expectations are shown to be petty in light of who He is.

> *The only expectation, the only hope that does not disappoint is the one we hold in God our Parent.*

God could arrange our lives so that nothing ever disappointed us, but instead He uses these experiences to remind us of our need for Him. He takes our pale and petty disappointments and uses them to fashion spectacular gifts, such as peace with ourselves and with others, patience as we walk through times of disappointment, wisdom to discern our unrealistic mindsets, perseverance to meet the challenges of future trials, and in the end, spiritual maturity (James 1:2–4).

All the while, our Father strengthens our understanding of the truth and establishes in us the faith that He alone is able to walk with us through every valley. What a rich legacy to pass to our children as they embark on their own journey through life.

- When you are disappointed in yourself, what are some of the emotions that arise? What do you think your children learn about you in these times? What are some potential positive lessons you could teach your children during times of personal disappointment? How would you communicate this to them?

- As you consider your children honestly, what disappoints you about them? Is it difficult for you to communicate your disappointment in their behavior without also communicating your disappointment in them as people? What is your plan for modeling the Father to your children the next time their behavior disappoints you?

- When your children are disappointed in others, how do they show it? How can you use these opportunities to teach your children about their need for God the Father, who never disappoints?

- What kinds of words will you use to talk with your child the next time he is hurt by a disappointment? How might you diffuse the emotion so that you can speak calmly to him about the expectations or actions that may have contributed to his disappointment?

Chapter Nine

THE OPPORTUNITY
OF A LIFETIME

E very family has its traditions, and I think the predictability of customs and practices are important to children. The problem with traditions is that you have to keep them up. Once begun, children expect them to continue regularly, without fail, no matter what. One such tradition in our family is watching the television show *Extreme Makeover: Home Edition* each and every Sunday evening. I don't even want to think about that inevitable day when the show has run its course and is no longer aired. There will be wailing and gnashing of teeth at our house!

One recent Sunday my son came in late and needed to be caught up on the story of the family getting the house makeover. His question was, "Okay, who's been maimed in this family?" You see, there's always some really sad story explaining why this particular family was chosen for the makeover—someone has died, someone has cancer, someone has been critically injured in a car accident. The show always begins with a tearful retelling of the recent trauma the family has endured. It occurred to me last Sunday that even though this show is produced to make money and even though the show leans heavily on the melodramatic and even though the tear-filled eyes of the design team members are a bit hard to believe at times—this is a really great show!

The show is charity, Hollywood-style. Yes, it's unrealistic and nothing they do can be reasonably replicated at home, but at its core the show is helping people in need. And based on the incredible success of the show, this appeals to millions of Americans. The desire to help others is part of the human condition—the good part. The show highlights the rush we get when we work together to help someone in need. The great and weighty urgency of the need makes us want to act immediately to help. There's great camaraderie in working charitably as a team. The overwhelming appreciation of the family when the house is finally revealed is intoxicating—we want to watch it over and over.

> *The desire to help others is part of the human condition—the good part.*

If you look closer, the show also shows some of the potential pitfalls of helping others. For example, the extravagance of completely destroying the family's old home and building an enormous new one can be overwhelming. The family is sent away on a vacation while their home is made over, so they are not involved at all in helping themselves. When we swoop in and take over in an effort to help a person or a family in need, we risk endangering their dignity, and we must be careful not to do this. We want to teach our children that helping people in need is not a hostile takeover; rather it is marked by mutual vulnerability in which everyone is blessed—those who need to be helped and those who need to help.

THE HUMAN CONDITION

We humans are designed for interdependence. We have to depend on one another for all sorts of things that are important to our emotional, financial, and even physical survival. As individuals we are weak and broken and vulnerable to all sorts of scariness, but when connected to each other, we are powerful. Clearly, this was God's intention when He created us. Our mutual dependence is a dance—you step toward me as you help to ease my pain, I step toward you as I give to meet your need. Back and forth we go, sometimes leading, sometimes responding, ever aware of our own needs but also of the needs of others who might join our dance for a time. This dance goes on in our social circles, in our communities and schools, in our churches, and in our families.

Being connected to others in mutual dependence is beautiful and invigorating, and at the same time, it can be frustrating and even painful. As much as we want to do life on our own, we just can't. At some point I will need you and at some other point you will need me. God's hope is that we will meet each other's needs with a sense of mutual respect and gratitude. He shows us this truth in an almost comical way in 1 Corinthians 12, where He says that if you're a foot and I'm an eye, neither of us will make it very far without the other (1 Corinthians 12:21–26).

In this perpetual state of interdependence, we have a directive from our Father. Not a suggestion, not a good idea, but a mandate: Practice charity. Serve those in need. Get outside of your comfort zone and put someone else's needs above your own. Take care of each other. Feed His sheep (John 21:15–17). And God goes a few steps further and says that our willingness to do this has everything to do with our love for Him.

Scripture is clear in many places that ministering to those in need is not an option for any believer or believing family. The most chilling illustration of this is the parable of the sheep and the goats (Mathew 25:31–46). In it Jesus explains that in the end times, when God separates those who knew Him and ministered to Him from those who didn't, there will be some big surprises. Those who declined to feed the hungry, to give drink to the thirsty, or to visit the sick are called "cursed" and thrown into the lake of fire. This seems a bit extreme given that we're talking about only a little food and drink and time. But Jesus is as clear as He could be about this. He is present with those in need, and a missed opportunity to minister to them is a missed opportunity to minister to Him.

The Father has always had a special place in His heart for the needy. It is the poor and needy who are often most aware of their need for Him, and He takes special care of them. But our children will not see this relationship God has with those in need unless we point it out to them. Children, like some adults, often equate God's love for people with His provision for them—i.e., if you are a good person, then God will give you lots of good stuff. They will see someone in need and assume that he is bad because God doesn't seem to be providing for him. We must do what we can as parents to dispel this myth.

H - E - L - P

To practice charity is to help others. While it is true that God intends for us to go outside of our comfort zones to help people in need, we must remember that this practice begins at home. Our children learn to have a heart for those in need when there is an atmosphere of kindness and willingness to help each other in our homes. For example, my daughter practices charity when she sees me at the door with an armload of groceries and rushes to help me. My son practices charity when he sees that some household chore needs to be done and asks if he can help. As we teach our children the virtues of charity, we build in them an awareness of the needs of others and a spirit of willingness to help. But we also must encourage in them a willingness to be helped as well.

Our children learn to have a heart for those in need when there is an atmosphere of kindness and willingness to help each other in our homes.

In many ways it is easier to give help than it is to receive help. When we give to others, we have more control than when we receive from others. Sometimes receiving help is awkward, and we often hear our children saying, "I can do it myself" or "I don't need help." Sometimes they don't need help, in which case we don't help them. Sometimes they don't want help even though they need it, in which case we wait to help them—preferably until they ask for it.

If we help our children when they don't need or want our

help, we're often doing it for ourselves and not for them. It is time-consuming and awkward to see our children struggle with a task we could so easily do for them. There is a fine line between needing help and simply needing to struggle through. We thwart our children's growth when we help them too much. This is not true help because they are not in true need. But when they are in need and ask for help, we must teach our children a gracious response to receiving help, to appreciating the efforts of others on their behalf. This will further their understanding of and appreciation for helping others—for charity.

The roots of charity are in helping and giving. Even children as young as four years old should have little chores and responsibilities around the house. This begins the groundwork for an understanding that the family works best in cooperation with one another. However, with specific assignments some children adopt the mentality that unless it's their job or their turn, they do not need to participate. Anytime children are asked to help, they must do so. If they choose to complain or do a poor job, they turn an opportunity for helping or giving into tedious work. And that's their choice, but either way they will help.

BEYOND HELP

Recently my daughter asked me if there were six zeros in the number one million. I said there were, and then asked her what she would do if she had a million dollars. I expected her to say she would buy a million cats, or something along those lines. Instead, she said she would keep one dollar and give the rest to the poor "because they need it more than me." It struck me that even at that young age she longs to make a difference in her world. Since I don't have a million dollars to give my daughter so she can practice charity, I can start by teaching her how to be sensitive to the needs of the people God has put in her world.

Children of all ages need opportunities to practice charity in its purest sense. These opportunities will be well received by most children because they long to help in some tangible way. Starting from a very young age, their senses of purpose and calling are forming rapidly. They want to go beyond just helping. They want to make a difference.

One of the most difficult aspects of charity for children to embrace, however, is generosity. Being generous with your help means not needing to be asked more than once, if at all. It means taking responsibility to help each other even if it is "not your turn." Generous charity is a result of being not only attuned to others but also willing to part with what we have. It gives us a chance to be free from the bondage of our things, our stuff. It is the embodiment of Philippians 2:4—looking "not only to [our] own interests, but also to the interests of others." But how can this be taught in a way that maintains the spirit of generosity rather than making it compulsory?

Sometimes you can't. Sometimes helping others will be compulsory for children. It's important for them to know that at times they will feel compassion and want to practice charity and at other times they will not. But whether they feel it or not isn't the point. God tells His children to do good to others "as we have opportunity" (Galatians 6:10)—not just when we feel like it or when it's convenient, but whenever an opportunity presents itself. Feeling charitable is a wonderful thing, but it's never a prerequisite to acting charitably.

*God tells His children to do good to others
"as we have opportunity," not just when
we feel like it or when it's convenient.*

An atmosphere of mutual help and giving—a charitable home—is one in which there is mutual respect. Perhaps you grew up in such a home; perhaps you did not. Now that you're a parent, you can choose to infuse respect in the atmosphere of your home. It's important to acknowledge, for example, when your children are helping, especially when they were not asked to do so. "Sam, you just ran right over here to help me, and I didn't even have to ask you. Thanks!" or "Sarah, you didn't have to volunteer to help, but you did. Thanks so much!" Making a habit of verbalizing your appreciation for each other's help and gifts models for children how to receive help and giving from others.

The charitable lifestyle is one in which giving and receiving—mutually helping one another—goes on in a natural ebb and flow. I remember my parents giving regularly to the local thrift store whenever they had a clothing drive. But rather than waiting to be asked for help, we can be aware of the needs of those around us. Many people give when the American Cancer Society calls or when the local mission has a fund drive. But our Father challenges us to a lifestyle of proactive—not reactive—giving of our time, our resources, and ourselves. This is the model we want our children to learn as they grow up so that it will be part of them.

The Dark Side of Charity

Ask your children what they think *charity* means. If they are young, they may have never heard of the word. If they are older, they might say that it's giving to the poor. Many of us have this definition of the word in our heads, too. We grew up believing that charity is what rich people practice toward poor people, what white people do for minorities, and what able-bodied people extend to the handicapped. Because of these generalizations and stereotypes, *charity* has taken on a negative meaning. I mean, who wants to see themselves on the receiving end of that? I don't want to see myself as "Tiny Tim"; I want to be Ebenezer Scrooge on Christmas morning!

Just like any other good and right practice, charity can be done in such a way that it actually becomes hurtful rather than helpful. For example, if you are in need of something and I give to you grudgingly, making it painfully clear that this is an imposition or a burden to me, then I have not practiced charity. If I give to you when it is convenient for me to do so, this is not true charity either. If I give to you expecting something in return—gratitude, indebtedness, paybacks— then I have not practiced charity. There is a sense of power that one feels when he helps or gives to another. That feeling of power can be enticing, but it is not what our Father had in mind when he told us to consider others more important than ourselves (Philippians 2:3).

People who have used charitable giving for self-serving and attention-getting reasons have tainted the practice. Our children need to know that even in Jesus' day, He had to warn the people against doing good works just so they could be seen

(Matthew 6:1–2). There is great spiritual reward in giving to others, unless we "sound the trumpets" to announce our giving, in which case getting noticed is all the reward we'll get. As we teach our children to hold in mind the needs of others, we also need to show them how to give to others in a pure way, unadulterated by pride and self-righteousness. When we help, we want to do so in a way that preserves the dignity of the one helped.

> *We need to show our children how to give to others in a pure way, unadulterated by pride and self-righteousness.*

But charity is not just the voluntary giving of money or help to people in need; it is also the willingness to see people with a sympathetic, tolerant, and favorable spirit. Interacting regularly with those in financial, physical, and emotional need helps to shatter the stereotypes we hold. Often when I give to people, I have to fight the urge to judge them—to judge their lifestyles or their choices, to judge the decision-making that got them into this predicament in the first place. If my self-righteous, know-it-all spirit eclipses my pure desire to give or serve, then I've sapped all the virtue out of the experience. When I finally lay down my judgments and stereotypes, I realize that the people receiving my help are not all that different from me.

We are told that religion at its purest is "to look after orphans and widows in their distress" (James 1:27). Why is this act hailed above all the millions of other ways we show our faith? Perhaps it's because there is no hope of a widow or an orphan paying us back. People in desperate need are in a unique position to minister to us. No, I don't have this backward. *They minister to us* by providing for us a chance to give unselfishly and to simply obey our Father when He tells us to serve. It is our duty and it is our privilege as God's children to give and to serve others.

But it's fun, too. It's fun to give and to serve together. Some of our favorite times as a family have been helping others when they were moving, hosting people in our home, and bringing food to families in need. The practice of charity is a celebration of the resources and gifts God has given our family. Our Father loves a cheerful giver, and we can model for our children being cheerful when we give, when we serve, and when we minister. When we give, we give freely. When we serve, we do so whole-heartedly and without complaining. When we minister to others, it's about them, not about us. So while it's important to take the practice seriously, it can also be a joyful experience.

Opportunity of a Lifetime

The practice of charity—with a full awareness of the pitfalls of abusing it—is a cornerstone of the development of compassion and empathy in our children. As our children grow in their sensitivities to the needs of others, they want to act. They want to serve and give and make a difference. Don't make the mistake of thinking that you have to go on a mission trip to practice real charity. Look around your community, in your church, in your neighborhood. I guarantee you will find someone in need.

It is this *lifestyle* of serving and giving that we want to cultivate in our children—not just the occasional fun mission experience, but the regular practice of giving to those in need. We want to give regularly of our time and our treasure, and I use *our* loosely. As the offertory plate was being passed in church one recent Sunday, I saw my son's plastic baggie of coins and dollars go by. On the baggie he had written "God's Dough" in big letters. How appropriate. How real. It *is* God's dough and God's time and God's treasure that we give.

> *It is this lifestyle of serving and giving*
> *that we want to cultivate in our children—*
> *not just the occasional fun mission experience.*

Take some time to think through what your family can do to participate in ministry to others on a regular basis. Check out opportunities at your church, but don't forget about opportunities in your community as well. A service opportunity doesn't have to have the "Christian" stamp on it to be ministry. How you behave as a family—how you represent your Father—is what makes it ministry.

Check out some of the possible ways your family can help others in need in your community. Yes, take a family mission trip if you can, but also—and more important—seek to honor your Father in the way your family gives and serves every day. Here are a few ideas to get you going:

- Deliver food to the needy or the homebound—and stay a while for a visit.

- Help clean up a nearby playground—and work hard until you're all exhausted.

- Spend time with some elderly folks in the nearby nursing home—and ask them about their families, their histories.

- Sponsor a child overseas—and let every member of your family pitch in.

- Provide some care for someone with special needs— and find out what *really* makes them special.

In putting any of these ideas into practice, you can model for your family not only the importance of giving help generously but also of receiving a blessing from those you intended to help.

Consider This...

- What are some ways you plan to teach your children to practice charity in the home?

- In what ways have you seen the practice of charity being misused? What was the effect on the recipient? on the giver?

- What charitable opportunities within your community or abroad has your family participated in? What did your children learn?

- What are some possible resources you could use to look into such opportunities?

Chapter Ten

THE ENTITLEMENT TRAP

...are endowed by their Creator with certain inalienable rights...

Maybe as a child you were required to memorize this portion of the Declaration of Independence. Thomas Jefferson, who penned these words, was keenly aware of the importance of rights, probably because he knew they came at such a high cost. As a citizen, I should both know and exercise my rights—and be ready to defend them if need be. "Stand up for your rights" is a challenge to resist oppression and accept our standing as free citizens in a free country.

Growing up, I had a clear understanding of what I thought to be my *rights*. I felt very much entitled to the nice things I had—plenty of clothes, a big house with a pool, a private education. I attended a university whose student population included children from some of the wealthiest families in the nation. So when my mother informed me that I would have to find a job to earn my spending money, I was appalled. I was shocked. I was speechless. All my friends at college had unlimited bank accounts. They thought nothing of running to the mall every weekend with Daddy's credit card. *That* was the life I was meant to lead, I thought.

Even now, I sometimes live as though there were a Christian Declaration of Independence that guarantees me the right to a successful life, the right to a strong marriage, to well-adjusted children, to a healthy body and a healthy bank account. My desire for success in my pursuits—career, marriage, child rearing—at some point becomes a sense of entitlement, as though God owes me success in return for my faithfulness. This view of life lies at the top of a slippery slope. When I begin to live in a contractual relationship with God—as though He owes me for my efforts—I have bought into the dangerous lie of entitlement, and without any doubt I will model this for my children.

> *When I begin to live as though God owes me for my efforts, I have bought into the dangerous lie of entitlement.*

ENTICING OUR CHILDREN INTO THE TRAP

Part of God's job as our Parent is to give us a healthy and true perspective of Himself and of ourselves in relation to Him. We tend to get this perspective skewed. In my own version of this arrangement, I live at the center of God's universe and He just happens to have the same plans for me that I have for myself. How convenient.

But in Romans 11, my Father reminds me that I will never fully understand Him or be able to give Him anything remotely equal to what He has given me. My Father's wisdom and knowledge know no bounds. His perspective on life is crystal clear. He needs no one to help Him make decisions or to assist Him in any way. What's more, there has never been a human who could understand God, who could help God, or who could repay God for what He has done (Romans 11:33–36). This is reality.

He has everything to offer me as His child, but I have nothing to offer Him. In short, God is not nor will He ever be obligated to me in any way. It is when I understand this that I recognize His extravagance in giving me undeserved favor, generous forgiveness, and every good and perfect gift that I have. My Father never loses sight of His position as God or of my position as His child.

On a much smaller scale, this arrangement is also true of the relationships we have within our families. Our children will never be able to repay us for our efforts on their behalf—the vast amounts of money spent, the sleepless nights, the never-ending plans and thoughts we have for them. Of course we would never expect them to repay us; these and all our gifts are freely given. Yet, it is easy to lose sight of our position as parents and believe we are somehow obligated to our children for more. We interact with our children as if we *owe* them round-the-clock entertainment. We owe them the coolest clothes. We owe them our wholehearted involvement in their extracurricular activities. We owe them an allowance, a college fund, and an inheritance. The truth is that these are gifts we may willingly give to our children, but they are not rights our children are entitled to; we must not lead them to believe otherwise.

We foster a sense of entitlement in our children when the

family is centered too heavily on them—their needs, their wants, their schedules. If we aspire to be super-parents, we can jeopardize a healthy balance within the family structure. It is easy to lose sight of the important distinction between what seems important to the children and what is best for the family. Many parents live as though these are one and the same. This fosters a strong sense of entitlement, which affects their attitudes in school, church, and almost any setting.

We foster a sense of entitlement in our children
when the family is centered too heavily
on them—their needs, their wants, their schedules.

We must not fail to teach them that the good in life is a gift—not a right, but a gift. Gratitude and humility are all but lost on our children's generation, and we have only ourselves to blame. Our super-parenting has spawned a generation or two of people who genuinely believe that life owes them success and happiness, regardless of their behavior.

Not a Right, but a Gift

Children should be able to count on such things as a safe home and food to eat. It's great for them to enjoy fun times and successful endeavors, too. The difference between enjoying the good things in life and expecting them is in the attitude. God is our Parent, and just like us, He enjoys giving His children good gifts. But also just like us, He is not pleased when His children demand gifts from Him or protest if a gift is not what they wanted. When people (including children) think something is rightfully theirs, they seek to control it, to manipulate it, to have it their way. What a contrast it is when instead they are given a gift and respond thankfully, perhaps pleasantly surprised and humbled.

How can we gain the perspective we need to see life as it really is, as a gift? What's more, how do we nurture this perspective in our children? In his book *Turn My Mourning into Dancing*, Henri Nouwen writes, "Prayer then becomes an attitude that sees the world not as something to be possessed but as a gift that speaks constantly of the Giver. It leads us out of the suffering that comes from insisting on doing things our way. It opens our hearts to receive."

Personal time in prayer is the avenue through which our attitude of entitlement is exposed as an ugly lie, and we remember our humble position with God. It is in times of prayer that we are freed to embrace God's plans, with no sense of personal rights or entitlement to sully our joy. As we pray with our children and model for them humility and thankfulness, they too begin to recognize that life—with all of its joy and sorrow—is God's gift to them.

FREEDOM FROM ENTITLEMENT

The most beautiful picture the Father gives us of a life lived free of the trappings of entitlement is that of His daughter Mary, the mother of Jesus. She was a virtuous young woman raised to love and respect God. She kept the laws of Moses and lived a faithful life. She and Joseph, her fiancé, were looking forward to a happy future, to children, to building a home together. Her visit from the angel announcing the coming of the virgin birth changed everything! It was a high honor, certainly, but it came with a price. All her dreams about how life would be, all her hopes of being a typical wife and mother, were gone in an instant. She was asked to walk a road no earthly parent would choose for a child—a road of difficulty, of anguish, and of shame—and yet in His sovereignty, her heavenly Parent chose it for her.

When Mary's life plans were so irrevocably snatched away, there was no crying out to God at the injustice of it all, there was no mourning over the life that could have been, that should have been. Mary's response was humility and praise (Luke 1:46–55). How could this be? Because hers was a life lived without entitlement, with no sense of violated rights, with hands open to God's plans. By comparison, my white-knuckled hold on the plans and dreams I have for my life and for my children is downright embarrassing.

Mary recognized the truth that so many of us fail to see—that we are not entitled to anything from God's hand. We have no rights to happiness or success or leisure or pleasure. We are not entitled to self-sufficiency or satisfaction in this life. We don't even have the right to the air we breathe. Our Father's gifts to us are just that—gifts. Gifts given freely and generously by a Parent who loves His children. Yet for most of us, if we don't get our weeklong family vacation each year or our annual bonus at work, we feel put-upon. If we have financial difficulties or have to go to marriage counseling, we cry, "Not fair!" If our child is diagnosed with a disability or a serious illness, we are shocked and appalled at the injustice. When life does not cooperate with our plans, we are more than disappointed and saddened; we are indignant. But these reactions are based on the false belief that we are entitled to some level of ease, comfort, and success in this life. God never promises this. In fact He has told us we might expect just the opposite (James 1:2–4).

> *We are not entitled to anything from God's hand.*
> *Our Father's gifts to us are just that—gifts.*

So how do we combat the spirit of entitlement in our children, and yet do so without limiting their options? Well, perhaps we can't. Maybe we can't combat such attitudes without closing some doors for our children. We must accept the idea that our child does not need to participate in every opportunity that presents itself. It can be a healthy experience for a child to hear the words "We can't afford it" or "This is not a good time" or simply "No."

This is even more effective when we do not feel the need to thoroughly explain and justify our decision. It is important to a child to know that he has been heard; however, when we take great pains to explain to our children why they cannot do something, we foster the expectation of an explanation every time they don't get their way. This can do more to encourage entitlement than simply allowing them to get their way in the first place.

Sometimes the answer is simply "no" with no bells and whistles. Sometimes it is "work it out between yourselves" when children want us to stop what we're doing and mediate their arguments. In my home, the statement "You are responsible for your own fun" has been the response to many an "I'm bored" or "There's nothing to do." Children develop a healthy respect for parents when they recognize that we have interests, activities, and responsibilities that have nothing to do with them. Every outing does not need to be a production; every day does not need to hold a party.

> *Children develop a healthy respect for parents when they recognize that we have interests, activities, and responsibilities that have nothing to do with them.*

A New Perspective

Landon's mother and father were tired of their ten-year-old's constant requests for new things. It had gotten so they couldn't even go to the grocery store without Landon pleading for his parents to buy him "just one thing." When Landon was younger, his whining and complaining on errands grew unbearable, so his parents began to promise him treats if he behaved himself in public. What started out as a short-term remedy to his negative behavior had grown into an expectation that he should receive a treat whenever he behaved himself. This sense of entitlement began to infuse other areas of Landon's life as well. When asked to do chores around the house, Landon asked what he would be paid for each chore. When Christmas rolled around, Landon's wish list was more of a shopping list for his parents. Landon's whining and complaining had simply been replaced by a new and more serious set of negative behaviors, with an attitude to match. Landon's parents never intended to create or encourage this sense of entitlement in him, yet they found themselves falling deeper and deeper into the patterns of promising him rewards for every good behavior.

If these patterns do not change, Landon is likely to have problems in a number of areas as he grows up. He has learned to expect positive attention for his negative behaviors, so he will use these as a means to get attention in school, in his friendships, and later in his adult relationships. His development of a healthy work ethic may be impaired, causing problems in his academic work and even in his extracurricular activities. The impression that he is entitled to special rewards for showing responsibility and obedience could easily sabotage his ability to pursue goals later in life.

When we parents use too many tangible rewards for good behavior, we diminish the benefits of the more important relational rewards. Parents give relational rewards by energetically connecting with their children in positive, encouraging ways. "Way to go! I knew you could do it!" "Wow, I really like the way you worked hard on that project!" Words of encouragement offered with the energy of positive emotion are pure gold to our children. A firm hand on the shoulder coupled with a smile, perhaps a high-five for younger children, will have the same positive results. Most important, relational rewards help our children develop a sense of satisfaction and joy in a hard job well done—a capacity that will serve them well as adults. These are the "treats" our children really have an appetite for.

I love my children, and because I love them I often stand in the way of their happiness. Sound heartless? There was a time when happiness to my son equated never having to take a bath. Needless to say, I made him bathe anyway. When my daughter was young she enjoyed eating only marshmallows. I made her eat healthy foods—even some she didn't enjoy. If I were to be solely concerned with their happiness, I would make very unwise decisions on my children's behalf. God our Parent loves us with a purity we cannot fully comprehend; His focus is not on what we think we need to make us happy. It is on making us ready for the greater adventures that living according to His plan brings. Likewise, we love our children in ways they do not understand. When we keep in mind the bigger goals of training our children's character, of encouraging their independence and resourcefulness, we make wiser decisions than when we feel compelled to provide for their immediate satisfaction and enjoyment.

> *When we keep in mind the bigger goals of training our children's character, we make wiser decisions than when we feel compelled to provide for their immediate satisfaction and enjoyment.*

THE BLESSING OF WORK

I chuckle now (though I didn't at the time) when I remember the sight of my then five-year-old daughter trudging down the stairs with a load of dirty clothes, saying indignantly, "I am not the maid, you know!" We didn't have a housekeeper, but she had heard this protest from her mother on occasion, and she wanted to register her indignation at having to bring down the laundry. What a picture of entitlement, pure and unadulterated! She did not appreciate being treated like hired help. She has since learned, however, that she, just like every other member of our family, is *unhired* help.

An effective antidote to a strong sense of entitlement is a strong sense of hard work. Requiring him to help around the home is always good for a child regardless of how he perceives it. Remember, our Parent is the Creator of work and of the satisfaction and joy that can come from a job well done. The book of Genesis tells how God Himself *worked* to create this world (Genesis 1:1–2:3). He assigned the job of taking care of this world to Adam and Eve long before sin had entered the picture (Genesis 1:26; 2:15). In Matthew 25, Jesus tells the Parable of the Talents, in which the servant who did not work to increase what he had been given was labeled "wicked" and "lazy" (Matthew 25:26). By contrast, the servants who worked diligently were praised as "good and faithful" (Matthew 25:21, 23). God our Parent not only intends for us to work, but also considers hard work a virtue and a privilege.

We parents often make the mistake of equating work with stress. We see our children are stressed by their homework, stressed by their extracurricular activities and their social pressures. While we are often reluctant to insist that they drop or limit an outside activity, we are often willing to back off from what we require of them at home. Exempting a child from regular chores with excuses like "He needs a little downtime" or "I just wanted to give him a break for a while" only serves to thwart the development of maturity, and consequently adds to the very stress we were trying to relieve.

Even when our requirements are appropriate, a youngster may struggle to get his chores done. He may have to put forth extra effort to fulfill his responsibilities. You may need to stand in the doorway and talk a child through the job he cannot seem to get done by himself. Nevertheless, we must not shield a child from reasonable chores. We may need to help our children develop a plan for accomplishing their tasks, but the tasks should remain *theirs* to accomplish. With time and training, they will learn to balance their responsibilities and even grow to enjoy the results of their well-done work.

It is a skewed picture when the parents work and the children are worked for, when the parents serve and the children are served, when the parents pay so the children can play. Chores, responsibilities, tasks—whatever label you choose—give children an honest perspective of life within the family. Everybody works and is worked for. Everybody serves and is served. Everybody pays so that everybody can play.

> *It is a skewed picture when the parents work and the children are worked for, when the parents serve and the children are served.*

Our Father calls us to take our place in His great family and contribute to its health and effectiveness, sometimes requiring us to forsake our individual rights. We prepare our children to be a part of the larger body of Christ by first teaching them how to work within their own family system, contributing what they can and sharing in both the work and the bounty of the family. When we encourage these contributions, we in turn discourage an unhealthy sense of entitlement.

Every home is organized differently and there is no one-size-fits-all plan for teaching children to contribute to the family. However, there are some guidelines for encouraging a healthy perspective on family responsibility and work. Beginning around three years old, every child needs to have at least one responsibility. Consider the common family activity of eating dinner. Even a three-year-old can carry the napkins or the silverware to the table before dinner. Older children can set the table, clear the table, load the dishwasher, and wipe down the table. Many children can even plan the menu, help with the shopping, and do some of the cooking. There are jobs enough for everyone found in this one simple activity.

For a younger child, the attention he receives for his work needs to center on his effort, his "hard work," and not so much on the outcome or quality of the work. His contribution to the family is appreciated, and he is also taught to appreciate the contributions of others. As the child matures, the assessment of his work grows to include his willingness to comply, the care with which he has worked, and the quality of its outcome. Regardless of a child's age, he needs to see that the job he does is directly helpful to the family in some way.

THOSE TO WHOM MUCH IS GIVEN

The prevailing attitude of our society is that those who have been given much can expect to be given more and more. Once we have experienced something good, we believe that we are entitled to it from then on. If we receive an unexpected bonus at work, we then expect it the next year. Parents pass the same idea on to their children, maybe inadvertently, but sometimes even intentionally. If we can afford a housekeeper, why should the kids have chores? If we can afford to buy her a car, why should she have to work for one? This idea that for those to whom much is given, little is expected, is in stark contrast to what God our Parent teaches His children.

> *The prevailing attitude of our society*
> *is that those who have been given much*
> *can expect to be given more and more.*

The norm in God's family is that *more* is expected of those who are given much. Christians are charged with the responsibility to use what we have been given to benefit others. God's mandate is clear: Those who are given much in financial resources are expected to give to the needs of others (1 Timothy 6:17–18). Those who are given much in emotional resources are expected to bear one another's burdens (Galatians 6:2). Those who are well-equipped to help people when they need it should work wholeheartedly (1 Peter 4:10–11). God trains us to see our resources as gifts, used primarily to benefit others, not as entitlements.

A Response of Gratitude

With a proper balance, in which both children and parents work to benefit the family, a natural atmosphere of gratitude and healthy interdependence replaces attitudes of entitlement. Gratitude, like love, is not just a feeling; it is a choice, and it is the antithesis of entitlement. We teach our children to be grateful—even when they don't *feel* grateful—by making gratitude a priority in the family. We can go beyond "say thank you for your present" and teach them that the heart of gratitude is a right sense of one's place in the world. Talking at the dinner table about events and people for whom we are thankful—about the blessings we have received from others and the blessing we have been to others—can give us an interesting peek into the minds of our children, while at the same time encouraging their sense of gratitude and our own.

As we parents mature in faith and dependence on our Father, we learn to be profoundly grateful for His provision, His gifts given so freely and undeservedly. We must look for opportunities to speak and model our gratitude in the presence of our children. Gratitude comes from recognizing that we are not entitled to the gifts this life holds; rather, we are undeserving of all that is pleasing and satisfying. As God draws us out of entitlement to a place of gratitude, we feel compelled to invite our children to follow us.

Consider This...

- What do you think your children feel that they deserve? How do they communicate this? Are there some ways you may be fueling this sense of entitlement? If so, what might they be?

- What are some ideas you can implement to encourage gratitude in your home that go beyond "Say 'thank you'"? How do you plan to put these ideas into practice?

- How, specifically, do your children work to benefit the family?

- What is God your Parent teaching you about your own struggles with entitlement? In what ways is He showing you that life is a gift to be freely enjoyed rather than a right or an entitlement?

Chapter Eleven

THE LOST ART
OF PATIENCE

O ur family almost escaped the video game phenome-
non. For years my husband and I preached the
dangers of video games to our children. In excess,
they are harmful to the social and language skills of children
and teenagers—and adults too, for that matter. We allowed
them to play in moderation at other people's homes, but self-
righteously drew the line at allowing one of those machines in
our house. But somehow, having a fourteen-year-old tends to
soften some of those parenting absolutes. So, on the advice of
a very wise man who mentors our son, we allowed him an electronic game player and a few games. I still don't think I was
completely wrong about video games. But in moderation, they
can be kind of fun.

One recent family night we decided to get a game we could
all play so we could share in this experience with our son. Because
we also have an eight-year-old, we decided on a children's game
that seemed easy enough…until I tried to play it. As far as I
could tell, this furry, catlike creature went around with a vacuum
cleaner sucking up appliances and other household objects to be
used at some future time to kill monsters. The cat then ran about

frantically spitting out refrigerators as he searched for the secret force field that would transport him to another level, where the vacuuming up and spitting out of appliances would continue.

Trying to play this video game brought back disturbing memories of learning to drive a stick-shift car. There were a lot of false starts and sudden stops. I couldn't get the cat to go in the direction I wanted, and he was forever bouncing into things. What's more, the voices of my children frantically coaching me from the sidelines sounded remarkably like the panicked voice of my mother during our ill-fated driving lessons. Instead of enjoying the experience with my family, I ended up queasy with motion sickness and had to be put to bed early.

In general though, when I hear my children talk about video games, I am disturbed on a number of levels. The most concerning of all aspects is the restart button. If the game is not going well for you, if you're losing or simply not progressing as you had hoped, no problem! You can simply press the handy-dandy restart button and all your problems will be over. You will magically appear at the beginning of the game again with no poor score on your record and nothing but high hopes for the future. My children call this a "do-over," and its casual use drives me nuts!

Wouldn't it be nice if we could "do-over" other things in life, beginning again with no record of previous poor performance to sully our reputations? Knowing that failure was not an option, we would surely be fearless and bold. No, actually we would be impulsive and thoughtless. If we could just restart any botched effort without consequences, we wouldn't learn to persevere through difficulties or make wise and thoughtful choices. We wouldn't have reason to consider other people or to ask for forgiveness. But the reality is, we cannot restart relationships. We cannot restart jobs. We cannot even restart what we've just said. Whenever children add, "Just kidding!" to the end of a misspoken statement, they are reaching for the restart button. This idea that we can take back something we've said or done without any repercussions has crept into the thought structure of our society. Since our children feel less need to practice patience in their endeavors, we parents have to be more purposeful in cultivating it.

> *If we could just restart any botched effort without consequences, we wouldn't learn to persevere through difficulties or make wise and thoughtful choices.*

God tells us to wait patiently on Him, yielding ourselves to His timing and orchestration of events (Psalm 40:1; Romans 8:25). We are told to be patient with one another in the same way that He is patient with us (Colossians 3:12–13; 1 Thessalonians 5:14). We are told to endure affliction and suffering, knowing that God has not forsaken us (Matthew 5:11–12; 1 Peter 3:14). Most important, we are told that the very nature of love is patient (1 Corinthians 13:4). If we love someone, we must adopt a posture of patience, for this is the model of our Father's love.

When I have to tell my children for the fourteenth time in a day not to leave their shoes in the hallway or to close the door behind them, I consider them lucky that their mother doesn't throttle them. But in my saner moments I realize that on my best days, when I concentrate my efforts on being patient with my wayward children, I don't even scratch the surface of the depth of patience my Father displays for me. To say that God is a patient parent is a vast understatement.

Choosing Patience

There are many ways for parents to teach their children the art of patience. However, it is critical that we reaffirm this truth: *We cannot teach our children patience if we are not pursuing it ourselves*. It absolutely will not happen. A child learns patience when he is treated with patience. A child grows frustrated and embittered when he is treated with intolerance and impatience. Period. You can read every parenting book on the market and employ all the latest tactics, but your child will learn about patience from you when you're late for school and he's taking too long to tie his shoes.

This being said, it is important to pinpoint those specific areas where you lack patience with your children and submit them to the Father. Is it when you're in a hurry? If so, then it's important to notice how often you're in a hurry. Is it when they mess up your plans? You have to ask yourself how committed you are to those plans. Is it when they act childishly? Perhaps you might note that they are, in fact, children.

We have daily opportunities, when our children are watching, to exercise patience. The bottleneck traffic when we're late, the seemingly inept salesperson, the rude waitress—all give us a clear option to take a deep breath and act with kindness. We model patience simply by being willing to wait instead of muscling our way through to our goal. By using kind words and a pleasant tone of voice in the face of frustration and delay, we speak volumes to our children about choosing patience.

> *By using kind words and a pleasant tone of voice in the face of frustration and delay, we speak volumes to our children about choosing patience.*

Probably the most difficult time to model this trait is when our child is angry and frustrated. Even though it makes little sense, we often become impatient in response to his frustration, thereby adding emotion to emotion—and so the cycle goes. If, on the other hand, we can choose patience in the face of his unrestrained behavior, this will set the tone and demonstrate for him an acceptable response to the situation.

Using a purposeful and level tone of voice, you can tell a child, "You're all right; take a deep breath," or "It's time to be quiet and think about what you're saying before you say it." In a matter-of-fact way, show the child that his impatience is actually making him more frustrated than the situation is. You might talk children through their frustration, or you may let them take a time-out to get themselves back together. However, it's better to avoid rescuing them or distracting them from the situation without really dealing with it. Otherwise, you will miss a wonderful chance to teach them how to maintain control of their emotions when they are upset or frustrated.

Teaching Patience

In *Charlie and the Chocolate Factory* by Roald Dahl, the children who get to go into the chocolate factory are each selfish in their own way (except for Charlie). One rich girl has a daddy who gives her whatever she wants, whenever she wants it. One rather plump boy loves to eat everything in sight, while another little boy wants to watch television all the time and do nothing else. One girl loves to chew gum all the time and brags about this talent to anyone who will listen. Each of the children in the story is especially selfish about something, and in the end this leads to each one being thrown out of the factory. Each child represents a different form of impatience—wanting what he or she wants, and wanting it *right now!*

Have you ever really wanted something you didn't get—a job, a date, a house—only to find out later that it was a good thing you didn't get it? This happens to me a lot, because "I want it now!" has sort of been my mantra in life. Consequently, God is forever having to withhold from me what I think I really want, really need, knowing it could be disastrous if I got it. I can now safely say that I'm glad I didn't get that med student I dated in college who ended up a philanderer, that beautiful house we bid on that turned out to be in a flood plain, or that job that paid so well but would have taken me away from my family.

In the same way, we parents often know that the things our children want *right now!* pale in comparison to what they will receive if they can just learn to wait. Children—and adults too, for that matter—easily settle for something less than what they want if they can have it immediately. The entire sales and advertising industries bank on this. We are barraged daily with enticements to "Get it now with 0% financing!" and "Don't wait—sale ends Friday!" Adults can sometimes see through these tactics but children cannot. A steady diet of this rhetoric takes its toll on them, and they begin to believe that getting whatever they can get right away is better than waiting for what they really want.

> *Children—and adults, for that matter—*
> *easily settle for something less than what they*
> *want if they can have it immediately.*

As we parent our children, being patient with them can be a simple matter of letting time have its beneficial effect in their lives. If our children are not ready to acquire a certain skill or trait, for instance, we must wait until they are ready. Not every situation needs to be dealt with right away. Sometimes a few more mistakes must be made, a little more frustration must be experienced before the child is ready to be taught. In these times we are patient and we pray for God's wisdom regarding our child's development and the timing of our interventions. Yet how difficult this is, in a world of TV sitcoms where every problem is solved within thirty minutes (minus commercial time). We feel compelled to intervene right away, to solve our children's problems, ease their hurts, and mediate their grievances.

We must be wise not to seek shortcuts in their development; we must never intervene in such a way that our children do not reap what they have sown. If they have sown arguments and strife with their friends, and their friends disappear for a time, we interrupt the benefits of cause and effect if we fill up their friendless time with other activities. Likewise, if a child is careless with his toys (or a teenager with his car) and breaks them, our replacing that possession spoils a perfect chance for the child to learn patience when he is without it. Natural consequences—natural in God's order—can be the most effective teacher of patience.

PATIENT WISDOM, WISE PATIENCE

When God is patient, it is not an end in itself; it is always a means to some greater end He has in mind. He realizes that His children often need the passage of time, the ripening of circumstances and understanding, in order to fulfill His purpose. Noah was about six hundred years old when the floodwaters finally came on the earth. God was working out His plan through Noah and his family, and all the parts of His plan had to come together. In the same way, God patiently waited for just the right time to talk to a middle-aged Moses about leading the Israelites out of slavery.

How did God know the right time to tell Noah about the ark or to talk to Moses about going to Egypt? He knew *when* because He knew *them*. In His neverending wisdom, God knows exactly what degree of patience will be needed to teach and correct, to show and encourage, to assign and direct each of His children, because He keeps His wise plan for each of us in the forefront of His mind. We must do the same with our children.

*In His neverending wisdom, God knows
exactly what degree of patience will be needed
to teach and correct, to show and encourage,
to assign and direct each of His children.*

In the fourth century, Saint Augustine described a sacred union: "Patience is the companion of wisdom." Indeed, without the wisdom to see the bigger plan, patience is at best absentmindedness; at worst, cowardice. If I allow a child's annoying behavior to continue it may be because I have a wise plan in mind for teaching the child through that behavior. On the other hand, it may be that I allow that behavior to continue simply because I am not paying attention. How often have you witnessed a child misbehaving in public and the child's parent seems to be off in another world? There is no wisdom involved in not paying attention. This is not patience. Or, I may let the child continue in that behavior because I am afraid to intervene. Children who are corrected infrequently tend to react strongly, sometimes violently, to admonishment, and parents may be tempted to let poor behavior continue rather than risk a scene. This, too, requires no wisdom, and is certainly not patience.

Proverbs 19:11 says that wisdom actually *gives us* patience. Under God's parenting, the older and wiser we get, the more patient we become. Why is this true? Perhaps because over the years we accumulate more experiences of our own failure. The more times we find ourselves humbled, the more understanding we become toward others in their frailties and shortcomings.

With patience, we submit to God's plan for the evolution of each individual—the wisdom He displays as He nurtures each person's maturity and development. This wisdom then starts the beautiful cycle toward patience all over again. God skillfully parents us in such a way that these two traits—patience and wisdom—work in tandem. Because He is wise, God is patient toward us. With patience, He acts wisely on our behalf.

As parents we hope to embody this balance of patience and wisdom, and we seek to model it for our children. Although we expect some level of wisdom to come with age and natural development, we all know adults who exhibit little wisdom. When we teach our children to be patient, we know that they grow in wisdom as well. When our children do not learn patience, but instead learn selfishness, pride, and impatience, they often grow to be unwise adults.

We have seen the natural result of this lack of patience, namely a lack of wisdom, as children grow to adulthood. The "I want it now" generation is up to its eyeballs in debt, reeling from broken relationships, and short on job capabilities due to lack of sound skills development. Disillusionment is often the result when a person fails to learn patience. Impulsively jumping from one pursuit to the next or from one relationship to the next, we never reach those levels of depth and intimacy that require time and patience. This kind of shallow living breeds discontent, dissatisfaction, and ultimately disillusionment. I realize this may sound like a gross generalization and you may not think it applies to your children, but the scenario plays itself out across every socio-economic level, in secular families and in Christian families. If your children are not expected to learn and practice patience in the small moments of life, they will not gain the wisdom they will need later for more important ventures.

When we are faithful in the small things—in the momentary opportunities we have to be patient, for instance—God trusts us to be faithful in bigger things. So it is with our children. When we teach them to practice patience in the small things, our children will be ready to meet the greater challenges of life with patience and wisdom.

The Beauty of Boredom

We parents are afraid of lots of things—kidnappers, drugs, negative influences on our children, global warming, boredom. Yes, we fear our children's boredom, if we believe that their boredom is our problem. "Mom, we're bored!" they whine, and we try to fill their idle hours with activities, lessons, electronic entertainment, and organized sports. In doing so, we communicate the idea that if they are bored, something must be done about it, that there is something inherently wrong with being bored. But boredom is a beautiful thing. Boredom trains children in ways no planned experience could. When we doggedly refuse to let our children's boredom become our responsibility, they learn how to be responsible for their own fun, for their intellects, and for their own patience. They discover within themselves unexplored levels of imagination and depths of resourcefulness and patience they didn't know existed.

Boredom is a beautiful thing. It trains children in ways no planned experience could.

It is not uncommon for parents to misread a child's boredom and resulting impatient behavior as something else altogether. For example, some parents report that their child is "bored" in school and therefore must be brighter than the rest of the class. Perhaps so, but it might also be that the child has not learned to be patient with the learning process and the dynamics of the classroom. When children have had little experience in being bored, it can feel painful to them. This leads some children, when they lose interest in an experience, to disconnect from it intellectually and emotionally. They don't know what else to do. However, when children are made to be responsible for their down time, and when they are held accountable for their attention and participation in the classroom, they develop the skills to override the desire to mentally check out when things aren't interesting.

Sometimes, instead of talking with children about patience, we can allow the natural opportunities that boredom brings to take effect. Rather than distracting them from their impatience or taking responsibility for their boredom, we give that responsibility back to them. We hold them to commitments such as practicing their musical instrument or their sport for a given time every day, even when they lose interest. We do not allow them to quit a difficult task until it is done. And we rarely intervene to help. If the child can do the task but is making it difficult because he is bored with it, we do him a disservice by intervening. Sometimes a child needs to feel the negative impact of his impatience in order to learn to be patient. But when the difficult job is finished, we celebrate with him a job well done.

Hope

Patience contains a vital element of hope. We have hope, in our patience, that the difficult situation will change, that the child will learn, that the suffering will eventually subside, that the affliction is part of God's plan to mold us into the likeness of Christ. Without such hope, our efforts at patience will be short-lived and frustrating. Without hope we cannot muster up enough patience to fill a thimble, much less to parent a child. True patience is accepting with hope that life develops at its own pace, in God's time, and there is nothing we can do to speed that up.

In light of this, remember that no amount of good parenting, exposure to educational experiences, or good discipline will hasten a child's basic development. These practices might teach the child some positive skills, but if a child is not developmentally ready to do something, he will not be able to do it. A child's brain develops at its own rate, based largely on chronological age. It has nothing to do with intelligence, morality, or work ethic. For example, it is unreasonable to expect a four-year-old to make his bed with military precision. No matter how smart he is, he doesn't have the manual dexterity, the planning abilities, or the experience to do this well. This doesn't mean he will never make his bed with precision; it just means he is not ready to do it right now.

We must be patient with our children's development as it cannot be rushed. We need to make sure that what we expect of our children's behavior, their academic performance, or athletic skill is in keeping with their developmental level. When our impatience for them to mature drives our expectations of them, we set the stage for frustration and exasperation. But if we release our children and their development to the Father who made them, then we are free to be present with them, not rushing them but watching for what God is bringing to pass.

When our impatience for our children
to mature drives our expectations of them,
we set the stage for frustration and exasperation.

God tends each of His children as a patient gardener. He turns over the soil, pulls the weeds, and protects against the aphids. He is patient because He can see the garden *as it will be* and not just as it is. He knows it's worth the wait. At any given time, if we pay close attention, we can see some attribute, some feature, budding in our child's personality. First it's faint and barely noticeable. Then it begins to make a regular appearance. Soon we recognize God's familiar hand nurturing this fledgling trait. If we are patient with the progress of our children's development, we will someday marvel at the growth and the beauty that emerges.

Consider This...

- What triggers impatience in you? Knowing this, how can you seek to develop patience in your own life and in your parenting? Be specific.

- How do you talk to your children about their impatience? What is your emotional response to their impatience? Does this help or hurt?

- What is your usual reaction to your child's boredom? What are some specific ways you can use her boredom to teach her about patience?

- What characteristics of your child's personality or intellect do you see God developing? In what ways can you show patience during this development process?

Chapter Twelve

MERCIFUL UNCERTAINTY

We all know that feeling of déjà vu, when you get the distinct impression that you've experienced this before. But in parenting I usually get a feeling of *vujà dé*—my word for that distinct feeling that I have *never* experienced this before.

It's *vujà dé* when my children ask me questions that I don't know the answers to and have never even considered in all of my forty-plus years! *Who invented cookies? Why does friction cause heat? Can you ever sit on your own lap?* I know the answer to that last one, but the follow-up question of *Why not?* stumps me. When these questions are posed, I answer in one of two ways: *You'll need to ask your dad* or *You'll have to Google that one*.

It's *vujà dé* when one of my children doesn't make a team or doesn't get a role in the play and is distraught. I don't know what to do. I hate that feeling. Sometimes it seems that the more I say, the worse I make it. If God would just tell me what to say—maybe write it in the mashed potatoes—I could handle it from there. But that place of uncertainty, when I'm at a total loss as to what to do or say, is not a place I like to be.

It was *vujà dé* when a young mother in our school community died following a tragic accident; we couldn't understand how this could happen. What do you say to a child in the face of such stark and inexplicable disaster? There is no greater fear in a child's heart than losing his parents. We often cite God's protection to reassure our kids, and then this tragedy happens to our friends. For her family and all those who loved her, the whole unfolding of events was covered in uncertainty—the LifeFlight to the hospital, the week in a coma, her death, and then the hardest question of all: How will her family and friends go on? No matter how much time we spend in uncertain situations, we never get used to it.

The Avoidance of All Things Uncertain

Organizers, Daytimers, Palm Pilots—keeping people organized and in control of their schedules is a billion dollar industry in the United States. We are downright obsessed with planning what will happen next in our lives. *Hate* is not too strong a word for how we feel about sudden, unwelcome events that interrupt our schedules and leave us wondering how to react. We all have those periods of feeling certain about our lives, our plans, our goals, but we share equally in those uncomfortable times when life throws us a curve ball.

> *Hate is not too strong a word for how we feel about sudden, unwelcome events that interrupt our schedules and leave us wondering how to react.*

When we don't know how to do something, when we are awkward or frustrated, what is our first response? *This stupid computer!* Feelings of uncertainty often come packaged with annoyance and irritation, particularly when our inability is costing us a lot of time and energy.

In the same way, being unsure of how to act when we're caught off guard or face an awkward social scene is equally unpleasant. Our feelings can range from embarrassment to outright anger. Remember that time someone put you on the spot, asking an unexpected question, and you were uncertain how to respond? It's as if time stands still. Your face gets hot and you try to gracefully back out of the situation, but whatever you do it seems you're sure to say something wrong. I think our children feel like that on some level a lot more often than we think. They are so socially awkward when they're young, and they are forever putting their little feet into their big mouths.

When some aspect of the future is in question—from what to do during spring break to where our next paycheck is coming from—our feelings of uncertainty can be agonizing. We want it resolved. We want all the loose ends tied up. When this doesn't happen readily, it can bring us to a place of fear. This is also true for our children. Most of their fear is rooted in uncertainty about the future—how they will perform, what will happen to them, how situations will turn out. Mentally playing out "what if" scenarios is one way both children and adults attempt to control an uncontrollable situation—the future.

We parents know and have experienced far more than our children, yet even we are often awkwardly uncertain. When we see those all-too-familiar traits of irritability, anger, and fear in our children, we can deduce that there is uncertainty afoot.

This part is not hard to figure out. The difficult part is helping them determine what to do with their uncertainty.

BE STILL AND KNOW

My children don't like to be uncertain. They like to know what will happen next and how things will turn out. I do, too. When they are frustrated or angry or fearful, my temptation is to relieve them by filling in the blanks, by telling them what will happen next. But I don't always know what will happen next. In fact, I *usually* don't know. So I look to my Father to remind me how He deals with His children in times of uncertainty.

Most of the time God doesn't relieve our uncertainty by telling us what's going to happen or what we should do in a given situation. Instead, He teaches us about *what we can and cannot be certain of.* As much as we'd like to deny it, the truth is that there is infinitely more that we *cannot* know than we *can* know. When I am uncertain and feeling fearful or angry, God says, "You don't need to be certain about this, but you can be certain about Me."

> *There is infinitely more that we cannot know than we can know.*

I tend to run around like the proverbial headless chicken; God says to be still. Be still and know—not be still and know what to do, what to say, what to plan, but know that He is God (Psalm 46:10). Period. But we parents want more, don't we? We want a plan, we want assurances, we want guarantees. And in

His way, God gives us a guarantee. He guarantees us that He is God. He asks us to trust Him to be the parent and to care for us, His children. He reminds us that even we, sinful and selfish as we are, love to take care of our children, so how much more will He, being perfect, care for us (Matthew 7:11)?

As our Father, God has to teach us all the time about what we can count on and what we cannot. As we grow up in Him, He teaches us to base our thinking on what is certain—on the truth. So often we want to go with what we feel or what we hope will be true, but He keeps bringing us back to Himself. He declares Himself to be "the way, the truth, and the life" (John 14:6). He is the path, the ultimate reality and the clarity of perspective we need as children and as parents. He calls us to be certain of what is certain and to arrange our lives accordingly.

CULTIVATING UNCERTAINTY

Our children are clueless most of the time. Some are more comfortable being clueless than others, and younger children have less of a need to be certain about things than older children do. Wherever our children are in their development, they will come upon times of uncertainty—when they begin a new school (or even a new school year in the same school), when they encounter a loss or even a death, when they find themselves ill-equipped for a class or a sports team.

As with their parents, uncertainty in children can create a fair amount of fear and frustration, so these are our clues that we need to talk with them. In matter-of-fact tones, during the normal course of each day, we can teach our children about what they can and cannot be certain of. For example, they can never be certain of other people's reactions or behavior, they cannot know how to do everything right the first time, they cannot control most circumstances in their lives. On the other hand, they can be certain of essentially three things: the laws of nature, your love for them, and God's love for them.

Some parents—and I put myself in this category at times—have a strong need to be certain, to be right, and to be sure of the future. Yes, this may be personality-driven in part; we type A personalities are usually moving so fast that we don't allow time for uncertainty. But when we act as if we must always be right, win the argument, know what's next, have a plan, be in control, we give our children the mistaken notion that it is always important to be certain about things, even though it is usually not even possible! We would do better to let our children see us being unsure. We would serve them well to model healthy and proper responses when we are caught off guard by life.

Even in our parenting, it's okay to be uncertain. We don't have to pretend for our children that we have all the answers or that everything we do is right. It's a balance between exercising authority in our children's lives and being vulnerable enough for them to see that we're not perfect. This is the line we must walk as parents because it is the truth. We are not perfect; we don't have all the answers. We don't even know all the questions! But God has called us to be the primary authority over our children, and we must never lay down that authority—even when we're uncertain.

We don't have to pretend for our children
that we have all the answers or that
everything we do is right.

LEARNING TO TRUST

Sometimes children go through a "lucky rabbit's foot" stage in which they are enamored with the idea of good luck. They may have a lucky number or a lucky shirt they like to wear for exams or ball games. We parents look at this and shake our heads at the childishness of it all. How ridiculous to trust in a number, a shirt, a dead rabbit's foot! Our Father says the same—but to us. How ridiculous it is, He says, for you to trust in your own understanding (Proverbs 3:5). How dangerous it is for you to trust in your income, your possessions, or your financial portfolios (Proverbs 23:4–5; 1 Timothy 6:7–10). How foolish it is for you to trust in your abilities and strength (Psalm 20:7). This is every bit as ridiculous as a lucky rabbit's foot, says the Father.

As we teach our children what is certain and what is not, we are teaching them where to put their trust. Trusting something or someone makes us feel safe. We need that. Our children need that. They need to feel the daily security of God's unfailing love and His unswerving intention to provide for them, to keep them safe. In times of uncertainty, when it seems that their little worlds have been rocked, they need to be reminded not only of God's love for them, but also of our love and devotion to them that remains constant, no matter what.

An important lesson for children to learn during times of uncertainty is that they can trust their parents. How sad it is to try to comfort a worried and upset child who will not believe your reassurances that everything will be all right. When there is a big decision to be made in the child's life, such as where he might go to school next year, the child needs to understand that capable adults who love him are going to make this decision wisely. Sometimes it's important to say, "You need to trust us. We love you and we are taking great care to make a wise decision for you." We don't need to convince them of our wisdom. We don't need to plead for their trust or explain our rationale. When the decision is ours to make, our children need to be reassured that they can trust us.

At the same time, we don't want to dismiss their fears or take personally their lack of trust in us. Often when children are uncertain and fearful, they simply need to be reassured. They don't need a lecture on their lack of faith. They just need to be reminded of the truth. It's important to give our children Scriptures that they hear over and over and that they keep in their hearts for times of uncertainty. Some may be: Proverbs 3:5—*I can trust God even when I don't understand what's happening*, Psalm 56:4—*I can trust God when I'm afraid*, and Psalm 33:11—*God has a good plan for me, and it's for sure.* We cannot be with our children all the time, but Scripture can.

When I pray for my children, I often pray that they may know the love their dad and I have for them and that they may know the love God has for them. *We want our children to be certain of what's certain, and to base their understanding and their trust on these truths.* Just as God has taught His children over the generations to be still and trust in what is certain—to know that He is God and that His love for them is sure—we teach our children to be still in their times of uncertainty, and to trust in what they know to be true. What's more, I want my children to know that it's okay to be uncertain. Uncertainty in itself is not a bad thing; it can just feel bad. But when the feelings of uncertainty give way to surrender, we feel free. We don't have to have all the answers for our children. It might be enough to say, "I don't know" or "I'm not sure." And when they are tossed by the wind and the waves of this world, sometimes our job is not to protect them from the storms but to point them to the lighthouse.

> *God has taught His children over the*
> *generations to be still and trust in*
> *what is certain—to know that He is God*
> *and that His love for them is sure.*

God's child Job was seriously tossed around. He was hurled into the sea of uncertainty. And his experience is a precious reminder to us and to our children of what is certain. Everything Job held dear—not just a few precious possessions or even one of his family members, but *everything*—was taken from him. I can imagine that the nagging question in Job's mind was *What next?*—the question that sometimes nags me. The uncertainty in Job's life was of the brand that brings sorrow and anguish and pain with it. I am sure God had His reasons for allowing all this suffering, and I can't help but think that one of them was so that I could tell my children where to put their trust. Job's dogged refusal to reject God and give up on life is the redemptive theme of this whole story, and it is one that every child should know. Job's certainty was not in his money or his livestock or his servants or his children or his wife, thankfully. He did not base his life and his decisions on any of these. He knew that he knew that he knew, that God was God and that he was His son. This would never change, no matter how dire the circumstances. This is what I want my children to know that they know that they know.

As we walk through the minefields of parenting, trying not to cause any major explosions or injuries to our children, we need to focus on what's for sure. Much of what we are told about raising children, much of the helpful advice of others, is conjecture. It may work; it may not. It may be best for our children; it may not be. How do we know? Many times we don't. But in times of parental uncertainty our Father has shown us what is certain. He is.

THE BATTLE IS NOT YOURS

In America, we have put our trust in education. Not necessarily in the educational system, but in the idea of education. We think that society's problems would be solved if people were just well-informed. We continue to hear that if we tell teenagers about the dangers of drug use, they will not use drugs. I'm thinking that one's not working. Twenty years ago, we thought that if we educated the public about AIDS, the epidemic could be contained, but that didn't prove true either. Yet there is something in each of us that thinks if we could just understand something, we could control it. We cling to the illusion that if we can be certain of things, we could be in control of them. The problem with this line of thinking in parenting is not just that we are unable to completely understand our children, but we're not even supposed to.

Many parents see their children as little extensions of themselves. When the child looks good, they look good. When the child fails, the parents have failed. But that is not God's model. When I fail, God doesn't look bad, I do! God is not dependent on me for His reputation—thank goodness. And we are not dependent on our children for our reputations. If our goal in parenting is to look good as a parent, we've missed the point entirely. Parenting is a calling, and just like in any other calling, we are working for God's approval, not for other people's (Colossians 3:23–24).

Our children are ours for only a brief time—just a blip on the screen of history. They are God's children for eternity, and we are asked to care for them while they are young and fragile. You would think that God would give them to us all grown up and strong and not so easily broken. But He doesn't. He trusts us with these frail little beings, tender and impressionable, perhaps so that we will more fully recognize our need for Him in this venture.

God trusts us with these frail little beings, tender and impressionable, perhaps so that we will more fully recognize our need for Him in this venture.

He calls us not to be perfect parents but to be wholly dependent on Him. Not to be a strong parent, but to "be strong in the Lord and in his mighty power" (Ephesians 6:10). My children need me to put down my little bag of parenting tricks and use the resources of my one true Parent, because what my children are up against—the struggle "against the rulers, against the authorities, against the powers of this dark world and against the spiritual forces of evil in the heavenly realms" (Ephesians 6:12)—is simply too much for me.

The Mercy of Uncertainty

I want to be a good parent to my children, and I know you do, too. Our children need us to be. And most important, our Father calls us to this. But what do we need to parent well? I know I need patience and faith. Sometimes I need better boundaries or more wisdom as I react to my children's indiscretions. At other times I need courage to do the right thing by my children even when it's hard. What do you need?

The beauty of parenting my children while at the same time being parented by my heavenly Father is that He has what I need. Not only does He have what I need, He *is* what I need. God is the Originator, the Embodiment, the Model and Source of everything I need to parent well. In my uncertainty as a parent—in the *vujà dé* experiences—My Father invites me to draw upon His boundless resources.

In those times that I need patience, for example, I need to remember that God is the original and only source of patience. Patience is perfectly displayed in His patience toward me. He has shown me how to react to my children's childishness by the way He reacts to my childishness. He models patience for me in the Scriptures and in my life. And finally, He is the source of all the patience I need. My intellect is not the source. My past experience is not the source. My own parents' example is not the source. God may use any of these to help, but He alone is the source of what I need.

So what do you need to parent your children today? Do you need patience, peace, unselfishness, wisdom, discernment, faith, skills, compassion, relationship, forgiveness, boundaries...all of the above? Me too. When you have a chance, make a list of the things you feel you need in order to parent well. What do you *really* need? Sometimes I think I just need more money or more time or a bigger house or less stress, and then I could be a really great parent. But God lovingly shows me over and over again that His grace—His presence, His wisdom, His parenting—is sufficient for me (2 Corinthians 12:9–10). Perhaps it is when I am at the end of my parental rope that God is happiest, because He knows that my next step is to turn toward Him.

> *Perhaps it is when I am at the end of my parental rope that God is happiest, because He knows that my next step is to turn toward Him.*

As a parent, even as a human being, uncertainty can be frustrating and debilitating, or it can be the door to freedom. In my Father's arms, I am free from needing to have all the answers. I am free from having to look like I know what I'm doing when I don't. I am free from the tyranny of needing to know what's going to happen next. I am free from the mandate that I do everything right. I am free to be a child—His child—just enjoying my Father, soaking in His love for me, and then turning around to shower that love on my children.

Consider This...

- When you feel uncertain about something, what is your typical reaction? How do your children respond to uncertainty? Is there any similarity between the way you react and how your children react?

- Think about several things you are uncertain about right now. What kinds of emotions are you feeling as a result of this uncertainty? Have you, like me, relied on some things that are not at all certain? What are they? How has God shifted your focus from these things?

- What specific Scriptures can you give your children that they can recite when they are uncertain? How can you help them to keep these in their hearts?

- What do you need right now to parent well? In what specific ways can you seek these things from your Parent?

CONCLUSION

What does it mean to parent well? My answer to that question changes daily, even hourly. The bad news is I don't have all the answers. The good news is I don't have all the answers, but I know Who does.

Even as a parent, we are still on the child end of the relationship we have with God our Father. Not only were we once children, we are now and will always be God's children. So we parent well by first allowing ourselves to be parented well by submitting to our Father, learning from Him, respecting His Word, and seeking to understand Him. In submitting to God, we more fully appreciate the awesome responsibility we hold when expecting our children to submit to us. As we know Him better, we will know ourselves and our children better. It is in respecting our Father that we learn to nurture and value the respect of our children. As we seek to understand Him and His ways, we will better understand our role as parents.

We will not parent perfectly. Even though you and I are parented perfectly by a perfect Father, we are not perfect. While this notion may discourage some, it has the potential to release us from unfair expectations we may have of ourselves as parents. We will make mistakes—it's part of the deal. If we never made mistakes in parenting it is unlikely that our children would grow up recognizing their need for God. It is in our brokenness and pain that we seek Him, and it will be the same for our children.

Parenting is a trust-walk—not trusting that the children will "turn out alright," but trusting that God is their God too and that His intentions for them far exceed ours. We want our children to recognize God's influence in their lives more than we want them to recognize our influence. We want them to have passion and energy for those pursuits God has planned for them, much more so than for the plans we have for them. We want them to grow in their dependence on Him as they grow independent from us.

At its core, our goal in parenting children is the same as God's goal in parenting us, and is best stated in Philippians 1:9–11:

And this is my prayer: that your love may abound more and more in knowledge and depth of insight, so that you may be able to discern what is best and may be pure and blameless until the day of Christ, filled with the fruit of righteousness that comes through Jesus Christ—to the glory and praise of God.

As our children develop in their insight and understanding of themselves, of this world, and of God, we hope their capacity to love grows more deeply as well. With this maturing love we trust that their discernment of what is worthy and pure and right will expand and broaden throughout their lives. We know that the fruit of righteousness that naturally results when a person is living in faith will be evident in their lives. And in the end, all of our efforts in parenting and all of their efforts in living faithfully will be for the purpose of bringing glory and honor to their Father in heaven.

Soli Deo Gloria
To God Alone Be the Glory

RECOMMENDED RESOURCES

L iterature is an effective way to communicate important themes to children. Often they are open to
talking about topics they have read about. You may
use the suggested readings for children to help your family
discuss the themes and ideas presented in this book.

Also, parents may find that reading and discussing a given
chapter raises further questions. The following suggested readings for parents will help you find some answers. In addition,
the listed websites provide valuable resources to parents seeking
to raise their children well.

My hope is that you read all the books—those written from
a Christian viewpoint as well as those with a secular perspective—with the discernment and wisdom that can come only
from the Father.

CHAPTER 1: THE FAMILY TREE

For the children:

> *The Patchwork Quilt* by Valerie Flournoy, Dial Books
> for Young Readers, 1985

A Year Down Under by Richard Peck, Puffin Books, 2000

For the parents:

Heirs of the Covenant by Susan Hunt, Good News Publishing, 1998

Chapter 2: A Life of Excellence

For the children:

I Love You the Purplest by Barbara Joosse, Chronicle Books, 1996

Call It Courage by Armstrong Sperry, Simon and Schuster, 1940

For the parents:

The Trouble with Perfect by Elisabeth Guthrie, Random House, 2002

Chapter 3: Drawing the Boundary Lines

For the children:

How to Behave and Why by Munro Leaf, HarperCollins Children's Books, 1946

Holes by Louis Sachar, Dell Yearling, 1998

For the parents:

Boundaries with Kids by Henry Cloud and John Townsend, Zondervan, 1998

Chapter 4: Life in Abundance

For the children:

Small Gifts in God's Hands by Max Lucado, Tommy Nelson, 2000

A Little Princess by Frances Hodgson Burnett, Harper
Collins, 1963

For the parents:

How Much Is Enough? by David Walsh, Marlowe and
Company, 2004

Chapter 5: The Lessons of Choice

For the children:

Sylvester and the Magic Pebble by William Steig,
Aladdin, 1969
Peter Pan by J. M. Barrie, Viking Penguin, 1991

For the parents:

Parenting with Love and Logic by Foster Cline and Jim
Fay, Piñon Press, 1990

Chapter 6: Surprised by Anger

For the children:

When Sophie Gets Angry—Really, Really Angry by Molly
Bang, Blue Sky Press, 1999
The Tales of Uncle Remus by Julius Lester, Puffin Books, 1987

For the parents:

The Anger Workbook for Christian Parents by Les Carter
and Frank Minirth, Jossey-Bass, 2004

Chapter 7: With My Whole Heart

For the children:

The Velveteen Rabbit by Margery Williams, Doubleday
Books for Young Readers, 1958

Charlotte's Web by E. B. White, HarperTrophy, 1952

For the parents:
> *Raising Your Children for Christ* by Andrew Murray, Whitaker House, 1984

Chapter 8: Growing Through Disappointment

For the children:
> *Alexander and the Terrible, Horrible, No Good, Very Bad Day* by Judith Viorst, Aladdin, 1972
>
> *The Story of My Life* by Helen Keller, Bantam Classics, 1990

For the parents:
> *Raising an Emotionally Intelligent Child* by John Gottman, Fireside, 1997

Chapter 9: The Opportunity of a Lifetime

For the children:
> *Amazing Days of Abby Hayes #12: Good Things Come In Small Packages* by Anne Mazer, Scholastic Paperbacks, 2003
>
> *A Christmas Carol* by Charles Dickens, Bantam Classics, 1986

For the parents:
> *The Giving Box: Create a Tradition of Giving with Your Children* by Fred Rogers, Running Press, 2000

Chapter 10: The Entitlement Trap

For the children:

> *The Quiltmaker's Gift* by Jeff Brumbeau and Gail De Marcken, Scholastic Press, 2001
>
> *The Door in the Wall* by Marguerite De Angeli, Bantam, Doubleday, Dell, 1949

For the parents:

> *Raising Self-Reliant Children in a Self-Indulgent World* by H. Stephen Glenn and Jane Nelsen, Prima Publishing, 2000

Chapter 11: The Lost Art of Patience

For the children:

> *The Carrot Seed* by Ruth Krauss, HarperFestival, 1993
>
> *Island of the Blue Dolphins* by Scott O'Dell, Yearling, 1987

For the parents:

> *Your Child's Growing Mind* by Jane Healy, Broadway Books, 1987

Chapter 12: Merciful Uncertainty

For the children:

> *If You Give a Mouse a Cookie* by Laura Joffe Numeroff, Laura Geringer, 1985
>
> *Around the World in Eighty Days* by Jules Verne, Scholastic Paperbacks, 1990

For the parents:

> *Making Children Mind Without Losing Yours* by Kevin Leman, Dell Publishers, 1984

ONLINE RESOURCES

Although this is not an exhaustive list of online resources, they each provide many links to other websites you might explore.

www.aacc.net—American Association of Christian Counselors

www.schwablearning.org—A Parent's Guide to Helping Kids with Learning Difficulties

www.parentnetassociation.org—National ParentNet Association

www.focusonyourchild.com—a division of Focus on the Family